the
GODDESS
GUIDE

PRIESTESS BRANDI AUSET

the

GODDESS
GUIDE

*Exploring the
Attributes
and
Correspondences
of the
Divine Feminine*

Llewellyn Publications
Woodbury, Minnesota

First Edition
First Printing, 2009

Book design by Steffani Sawyer
Cover art © 2009 PhotoDisk
Cover design by Ellen Dahl
Editing by Brett Fechheimer

Llewellyn is a registered trademark of Llewellyn Worldwide, Ltd.

Library of Congress Cataloging-in-Publication Data

Auset, Brandi, 1978–
  The goddess guide : exploring the attributes and correspondences of
the divine feminine / Brandi Nicole Auset. — 1st ed.
      p. cm.
  Includes bibliographical references and index.
  ISBN 978-0-7387-1551-3
  1. Goddess religion. I. Title.
  BL473.5.A95 2009
  202'.114—dc22
                                        2009003857

Llewellyn Publications
A Division of Llewellyn Worldwide, Ltd.
2143 Wooddale Drive, Dept. 978-0-7387-1551-3
Woodbury, Minnesota 55125-2989, U.S.A.
www.llewellyn.com

Printed in the United States of America

To Dolores, whose loving spirit strengthens me each and every day
To Liza, who gave me an inspirational home
To Brian, who made sure I never gave up hope
And to all the mortal goddesses,
wherever you are

CONTENTS

INTRODUCTION

The study of the Goddess, and the integration of Her wisdom and glory into daily life, is a spiritual path—one of faith, love, and dedication. Each step along this winding, twisting trail leads to greater wonders; each question answered leads to twenty more inquiries; and in every face of the Goddess discovered, we find a reflection of our own souls.

All things are Goddess, and all goddesses are one Goddess. Like a large, well-cut diamond, each facet of the Goddess is a new face, a fresh aspect; but ultimately, every side is a shining, sparkling part of the whole.

We as humans, with these minds in these bodies, existing on this plane in a world so full of grief and suffering, find it difficult to ascertain the greatness of the Goddess. She is, after all, the Wondrous Divine, the Unexplainable, the Unknowable, the All and the Nothing. People can only have faith in that which they identify with, whether it is an idea for their future or the Divine Presence.

So how do we make the unfathomable, fathomable?

Each culture throughout the world has infinite lists of goddesses, for endless purposes, for exactly this reason. We need something to connect us to the Divine Presence, and the breaking down of the Goddess's powers and aspects helps us to identify and connect to that presence. We study Her, breaking down the Goddess like a complicated algebra problem; we divide Her into pieces we can understand, categories we can relate to, and name that chapter *Lakshmi*, or *Kuan Yin*, or countless others, in order to claim Her as our own.

I am a Goddess woman—always have been, even before I knew who the Goddess was. For as long as I can remember, I've always wanted a life outside of the ordinary. In my early teens, the discovery of a local New Age store called Good Scents started me on that path. As soon I as walked in, the scents of sage and Nag Champa captured my senses; and upon seeing the smiling, wise faces of the women inside, I knew I was home. The shelves were filled with crystals I had never seen, herbs I had never smelled, and books I had never heard of—but nevertheless, I felt a humming inside my heart, and the voices I had heard since I was a child said softly, "This is it, you found it, this is where you are supposed to be!"

I talked to Donna, the owner of the store and a "Witch extraordinaire." I remember feeling sheepish and embarrassed, asking her question after question: "What exactly is a Witch? What does *Wicca* mean? How come I've never heard of the Goddess? Why would anyone want to wear patchouli oil? It stinks!"

Donna was patient and complete in her answers, though a little distant. She kept staring at me with this slight grin on her face, which made it seem as though she was trying not to laugh in my face. Just as I started to feel even more self-conscious, she said, "The Goddess speaks to you."

"Huh?"

"The voices you hear. You do hear them, don't you?"

"Uh, yeah . . ."

"Well, that's the Goddess. One voice for each face that speaks to you. You dream a lot, too, huh? And then the dreams happen in your life, right? And sometimes you dream about yourself, but it doesn't look like you, and it's a different time and place, right?"

"I just thought maybe I was a little crazy, like I needed a pill or something."

"What are you doing in those dreams?" Donna asked me.

"Usually I'm in some long robe, in a forest or something, dancing and talking to a group of women. Sometimes, I'm running around like Xena, Warrior Princess, kicking a lot of ass."

She laughed and said, "Yeah, most of us think we're crazy, at first. You're not crazy. You have a gift, and if you came in here you're ready to start learning about it . . ."

Donna then led me on a tour through her store, recommending books and magazines, and referring me to various lightworkers and practitioners.

From that day on, "professional Witch" was my dream job. I imagined myself spending leisurely days on an island compound, being fanned with palm leaves by well-oiled men in thongs, feared and revered by the natives for my "magickal powers"; other days I saw myself dressed to the nines in the middle of a New Orleans cemetery, scaring the tourists with tales of how I made the dead walk as I held flames in my hands and laughed like a lunatic.

I admit I had an overactive imagination, as well as a blatant misunderstanding of what my path was.

My next few years were spent learning about the Goddess, devouring any book I could get my hands on, and studying various feminine traditions under anyone who would teach me. My connection to Her was fierce and loyal. I spoke to Her daily, as a trusted friend, a mother, a teacher, my Creatrix. I found the more I spoke to Her, the more I believed She was there, listening and caring for me; the more I believed, the louder Her answers became—first, in whispers of the wind and in subtle dreams, then in voice, as my clairaudient abilities began to unfold.

Now, fifteen years later, my dream is being realized, but in a completely different way than I ever imagined. Maybe it was the responsibility of adulthood—bills, relationships, morality, and so on—that grounded and centered me. Or perhaps it was the swift kick in the butt my mother gave me after I turned eighteen. (To quote her: "You are grown and you've got to get a job, because if you think I'm going to continue to pay for all these black clothes and candles, you are out of your mind!") But I think it was the development of my connection to Spirit, the realization of what walking the path of "professional Witch" really means. Those are definitely things my teenage mind couldn't process at the time.

The harder I pushed to be dark, tragic, and dramatic, the harder the Goddess pushed me into accepting the light of happiness. The more I tried to just take care of me, the more I was placed in a position to help others. I was so caught up in me, and what I thought I wanted, that I kept missing my true calling—as a teacher, a healer, and a woman. I kept missing that it wasn't so much a path of "professional Witch," but more the Path of the Blessed.

The drama queen in me wants to tell a story like, "I was visited by seven angels, my four animal guides, and this little green faery in a meditation, and they told me that I am Joan of Arc reincarnated and it's my destiny to change the world," but that's not the truth.

The truth is that I don't know when it happened, this embracing of myself and the Goddess within me. I just know that one day, the fantasies of a life like an occult movie just didn't appease me anymore. That one day, I took a nice, deep breath, and started thinking about why I could do the things I do, see what I see, hear what I hear. That all of a sudden, all the things my teachers had been saying, every lesson instilled in me, just made sense. It just clicked. And that inner voice, the one I had been ignoring for so long, said clear as day, "It's time."

And that's when the hunger came on me. It's a hungry passion, this need to help women change their lives, to realize the gloriousness that is them in all their being; to help heal those who can't heal themselves. And through this work, I've come to realize that my life is not about me—and it never has been, no matter how hard I tried to change that fact. My life is about how Goddess works through me. My purpose is to bless others until all the families of the world have been blessed. My truth is that I am just the vessel, the flute to be played by

Goddess in whatever way She sees fit. Instead of world domination, now my goal is, how can I best serve the world? How can I do what Spirit wants me to do without doubt, without questioning?

The surrendering of myself to Spirit, trusting Goddess to lead and guide me to do Her work, is how I truly claimed myself and my path. Not to say it's been easy, because it hasn't been. I still struggle with faith sometimes; I still complain when She tells me to do something I don't want to do. Anyone who walks a spiritual path has the *Why can't I just go back to the way I used to be?* thought every once in a while. Continuing to walk the path of light, with all of its experiences, is the hardest thing some of us will ever have to do. But our faithfulness, our open hearts, and our light make a difference every day in every person we meet. *We* are the ones who will change the world. *We* are the ones who teach. *We* are the ones who heal.

I'm still learning every day, as we all are, but I know that I am exactly where I'm supposed to be. And every day I give thanks for that Light that follows me wherever I go.

✳   ✳   ✳

The idea for this book first came in the summer of 2006. I was working full time as a spiritual counselor and a Reiki Master Teacher—a blessing, as I had spent the previous decade reading Tarot cards and practicing energy work as a part-time hobby. During my sessions I would always speak to the Goddess, deciphering the information She gave about my clients and their needs. Eventually I was invoking specific goddesses in my clients' sessions, allowing whatever aspect of Her that my clients needed to work through me in order to heal and empower my clients.

Before each session I would review my client's history and sit in meditation, asking for the specific aspect of the Goddess that would help heal my client to come forward. Many times I was visited by Goddess figures I didn't recognize, or could not determine; other times I would know exactly what the client's issue was, but have no clue about a Goddess facet I could invoke. I kept thinking, *I really need to make a list of all the different goddesses, and organize it by what they rule over! There is no book that does that the way I need it done!*

Many Goddess-worshipping women I knew where having similar issues. Friends preparing for ritual or personal study would ask me if I knew of a Goddess aspect that ruled over birth control, or one who liked turtles, or a Slavic goddess whose color was orange . . . basically, information that wasn't readily available unless you had Internet access, a library card, and about eight hours to kill. It was a seemingly endless line of questioning, which started the seemingly endless chanting in my head: *you need to write the book, you need to write the book . . .*

Like a bratty six-year-old, I refused. I couldn't fathom that I—with the attention span of a hyperactive monkey—was supposed to sit down and compose a reference book for the Goddess. I came up with excuse after pathetic excuse.

I'm too busy.

Writing a book takes too much time.

I don't want to, and you can't make me!

Can't I just suggest to other people that *they* write it?

It was only after three months of constant phone calls from the Goddess women, and incessant chatter in my brain, that I realized Spirit, like any loving parent, wasn't giving up on me so easily. The goddesses were going to keep suggesting, keep hinting, and keep talking until I did what I was told. Once I stopped fighting, and allowed myself to flow with the journey they were taking me on, I found the studying, gathering, and arranging of materials in this text to be one of the most fulfilling experiences of my entire life.

Hence, this book was born.

The main purpose of *The Goddess Guide* is for you to be able to easily define the influence of the goddess you intend to call for ritual and prayer. It is also an introductory reference for anyone with a curiosity about the Divine Feminine as She walks our planet. You may consult the goddesses as metaphors of feminine archetypes that live within you, and consider aspects you would like to invite, encourage, or dismantle in your own life.

While there are over four hundred goddesses in this book, it is by no means complete. The Divine figures herein are the ones who came to me specifically, through research and meditation. Each goddess was chosen based on the amount of information I could find about her, and how well I was able to connect with her essence in spellwork and ritual work. Goddesses not included in this text either have too little information on them readily available for further study or are too obscure to be used in New Age and holistic work. There were no barriers in my research—I examined the classics of Starhawk, D. J. Conway, and other spirituality greats; scoured the Internet; visited museums; and interviewed Goddess-worshipping women and High Priestesses in order to assemble the most information I could. I then molded everything I had learned into one solid resource, focusing on the basic overlaps of information.

No exact traditions of Paganism or mainstream religions are highlighted within this book; it is an accumulation of my spiritual wisdom and the factual knowledge found in my studies. The correspondences and descriptions of the goddesses are widely agreed upon, and certain attributes (colors and elements) have been expanded upon based on the psychological theories of Carl Jung, consensus in New Age spirituality, and my own personal experience.

I have chosen to arrange this book largely as a cross-reference, under the assumption that those who browse its pages have a basis in Goddess spirituality, and will be inspired to do further research on their own. In addition, the goddess definition pages give a basic overview of information about each specific goddess, including attributes, mythology, and how she is honored.

When dealing with the region and culture of each goddess, I have given as much information as possible, and included as many cultures as possible. The Goddess is every color, every shade and hue, and this text is meant to expose you to the many global traditions She is embodied within, as well as to open your mind to cultures to which you previously may not have been able to relate.

The worship of many feminine Divine figures spread throughout countless lands and civilizations, with many overlaps; there are instances in which goddesses are best described by the larger territory they inhabited, as opposed to a specific land, city, or ethnic group. For example, a goddess's worship may have been centrally Slavic, but her presence was also felt throughout the surrounding regions; in instances such as these, I felt using *Eastern European* as a cultural descriptor was better suited than the more limiting *Slavic*. (This example illustrates descriptions of Mesopotamian goddesses as well.) In Celtic regions, some goddess figures were worshipped in specific lands like Ireland or Scotland, but others were adopted by most, if not all, civilizations within the area, and are therefore better categorized with the broader term *Celtic*. The same can be said of those goddesses I list under other admittedly expansive descriptors, such as *Northern European*. The myths and symbolic information illustrating each figure are the ones I found to be most reflective of each goddess within her culture.

Use the book however it will best serve you. You can examine the content from cover to cover, or focus your learning on specific attributes needed for rituals, spellworks, celebrations, and healing ceremonies. You can study each section on its own, or cross-reference it with other chapters, in order to gain the fullest experience and wisdom.

There is not one "correct" way to commune with the Goddess. We all have our own private relationship with Her, our own special needs and sensitivities. Call Her name, know Her power, and She will make Herself known to you. Whether you entitle Her *Isis*, *Druantia*, or *Yemaya*; *Hina*, *Artemis*, or *Shekina*; the Goddess walks the path with you, leading and guiding you to that which will make you whole.

ONE

· · · · · · · · · · ❋ · · · · · · · · · · ·

The Goddesses

Abundantia: Roman goddess of prosperity, luck, and abundance. She is the personification of wealth and riches, blessing all who ask to receive her gifts. She is usually depicted as a beautiful maiden carrying a cornucopia from which she distributes food and money. Her image was found on the coins of Roman emperors, and she is known to gamblers as "Lady Fortune" or "Lady Luck."

Acpaxapo: Mesoamerican goddess of intuition. Among the Otomi people of Mexico, Acpaxapo is depicted as a serpent with the face and hair of a woman. She speaks through her followers, delivering messages, omens, and predictions of the future.

Agemem: Creatrix goddess of the Philippines. Agemem and her husband Kadaklan conceived the universe, and are the creators of the sun, the moon, the stars, and the earth.

Aglaia: Greek goddess of splendor. As one of the Three Graces, Aglaia is a spirit of vegetation and springtime. She is often depicted dancing in a circle with her two sisters, Euphrosyne and Thalia. She teaches her followers to adorn themselves in beauty and grandeur as a way of tribute.

Aha Njoku: West African goddess of yams. To the Ibo people of Nigeria, Aha Njoku is responsible for the creation and cultivation of yams, a main staple of their diet. She watches over the harvest of the vegetable and protects the women who care for the yams.

Aida Wedo: West African goddess of rainbows. Worshipped in Yoruban and Voudoun traditions, Aida Wedo appears as the rainbow python, a serpent whose scales are iridescent. Her rainbow body wraps around the earth and the seas, making her a cosmic protector and the power that links heaven and earth. She rules water, wind, fire, rainbows, and serpents. A benevolent being, she teaches her followers integrity, strength, and integration of the mind, body, and spirit. Her color is white, as it is the materialization of all colors, and she is traditionally offered rice, eggs, and milk by her devotees.

Aine: Irish goddess of love. Also known as the Faery Queen of Munster, Aine is aligned with faeries and the magick of the forest. Her name comes from the ancient Gaelic word *an,* meaning "bright." She is a moon goddess who inspires and encourages passionate love between woman and man, and is worshipped for her powers of fertility and healing. As the Dark Maiden, she is vengeful when crossed, defending scorned lovers and exacting revenge on those she feels are unsuitable mates. The feast of Midsummer is held in her honor.

Airmed: Irish goddess of healing. Airmed is a goddess of the Tuatha Dé Danann, who healed those injured in wars and battles. She collects and organizes herbs for health and healing, and teaches her followers the craft of plant medicine. She guards the secret wells, springs, and rivers of healing, and is worshipped as a goddess of Witchcraft and magick.

Aja: West African goddess of forests. Aja is worshipped throughout Nigeria and in the New World Yoruban tradition as a wise woman and healer. She rules over forests, woodlands, and the medicinal herbs found within them. She teaches herb lore to her followers, ensuring their physical and spiritual health.

Aje: West African goddess of wealth. As ruler of wealth in all its forms, Aje is widely worshipped. Known mainly through Yoruban and Voudoun traditions, she is sometimes depicted as a fowl scratching at the dirt. She is cool and calm, patiently guiding those in need of material prosperity. Capitalism, profit, and business all fall under her rule.

Akewa: South American goddess of the sun. The Toba people of Argentina worship Akewa as the sun and a woman of war. She is a sister and protector of all earthbound women, saving them from the captivity of patriarchal rule. Each day she travels across the sky, warding off demons with her bright rays of light.

Akhushtal: Mesoamerican goddess of childbirth. In the Mayan tradition, Akhushtal rules over the act of birthing, from conception to delivery. She is the patroness of midwives.

The Akkan: Life goddesses of eastern Europe. The Akkan are a quadrinity of goddesses who rule all aspects of life, including conception, birth, and destiny. These four goddesses work together to select a soul and place it into a body, then into the mother's womb. Their names are Madderakka, Sarakka, Juksakka, and Ugsakka. Madderakka is thought to be the mother of the other three deities.

Akonadi: West African goddess of justice. Akonadi is primarily worshipped in Ghana, but she is revered throughout most of West Africa. She is the Oracle, the speaker of truths seen and unseen. She uses her second sight to bestow justice on all situations, but she is particular to women and their troubles.

Akwaba, also *Akuaba:* Mothering goddess of Africa. The Ashanti people of Ghana place images of Akwaba over doorways as a symbol of welcome, ensuring the visitor will be well cared for upon entering the home. Young girls of maidenhood receive her image as gifts when they begin to menstruate, a sign that they are being welcomed into motherhood. Akwaba ensures that women can conceive without difficulties, and that pregnant women give birth to healthy, attractive children.

Ala: West African goddess of the earth. Ala is a goddess of the Ibo people in Nigeria. She is the Mother of All Things, as well as the goddess of death. She gives birth to the beginning of all existence, and as ruler of the underworld, welcomes the souls of the dead back into her womb. Ala despises any murderous act, which she considers a disruption of the natural flow of life and death. Her symbol is the crescent moon, and her temples are usually erected in the center of villages, complete with her image as a seated woman holding a small child.

Alemona: Roman goddess of the unborn. Alemona is the protector of a mother's womb, nourishing and guarding the fetus until she or he is ready to be born into the world. She safely guides the child from the spiritual, ethereal world into physical form, promising health and security.

Al-Lat: Arabian supreme goddess. *Al-Lat* translates simply as "the Goddess." She forms a triad with al-Uzza and Manat; they were worshipped throughout pre-Islamic Arabia. She is the feminine version of Allah, and is even mentioned in the Qur'an as one of the three "daughters of God." Oaths in Mecca were sealed with the vow "By the salt, by the fire, and by al-Lat, who is the greatest of all." She is the ultimate Earth Mother, providing her desert children with nourishment as it is needed. Her symbols are the sun disc cradled by the crescent moon, and square-shaped stones and crystals. Her sacred number is seven.

Al-Uzza: The Virgin Warrior of Arabia. Al-Uzza is the youngest of the pre-Islamic triad, with her sisters al-Lat and Manat. Referred to as "the Most Mighty," she is a fierce warrior in any battle, aggressively protecting that which she claims as her own. She is the ruler of fertility and wild beasts, and at one time she received blood sacrifices of animals and humans. Her role as the morning and evening star gives her power over astrology and the changing of seasons. As the goddess of the sea, she is the guardian of fish and dolphins, and her name is invoked by travelers and sailors for safe journeys. Al-Uzza's symbols include the acacia tree, clocks and timepieces, square-shaped stones, and granite. Cows, felines, and dolphins are sacred to her.

Amashilamma: Sumerian fertility goddess. Usually depicted as a cow, Amashilamma blessed the people of Sumer with prosperity and fertile lands.

Amaterasu Omikami: Japanese goddess of the sun. As ruler of the High Plain of Heaven, Amaterasu is the central figure of the Shinto pantheon. She is the highest manifestation of the universe, her radiance shining its life-giving rays over her people and the earth. Her beauty and light are all-encompassing, producing fertile fields of rice, wheat, and flowers. Her most popular and prevalent myth tells of when Amaterasu, overcome with grief, hid herself away in a dark cave, causing the world to be plunged into darkness and despair. Only the mirror reflection of her exuberance and glory was powerful enough to draw her out of hiding. She is the inventor of weaving and spinning, and is represented by the mirror.

Anahit: Armenian goddess of fertility. Anahit was a main deity in Armenia, ruling fertility and birth. Once viewed as a war goddess, she is the protector of the land and its inhabitants, and most of her images were created from gold. As she is also a goddess of beauty and water, doves and roses were often offered to her sacred images. In ancient Persia, Anahit was worshipped as the goddess of the Sacred Feminine, ruling dance, music, semen, and sacred prostitution. Throughout history Anahit has been compared to Artemis and Aphrodite.

Ananke: Greek goddess of attachments. Ananke materialized at the beginning of time with her mate Chronos, their ethereal bodies intertwined and coiled around the primal egg of the universe. After they split the egg into the separate parts of heaven, earth, and sea, Ananke and Chronos remained entangled as the Cosmos, representing time and the driving force of the universe. Ananke became the aspect of necessity, ruling compulsion and all forms of slavery and ties, including the bonds of friendships and love. Her name was often evoked by prisoners and slaves seeking freedom.

Anapel: Siberian goddess of birth. Known as "Little Grandmother," Anapel is the sovereign of origins and new beginnings. In her role as fate and destiny, she chooses the body and life path each soul will reincarnate into. Worshipped by the Koryak people of Siberia, Anapel is celebrated at the birth of a child.

Anath: Canaanite goddess of love and war. Anath is the Virgin, Mother, Warrior, and Wanton, and was worshipped throughout Mesopotamia. Her name means "to answer," "strength of life," or "active will." Her brother and consort is the god Ba'al, or Bel. She has a ferocious appetite for sex and blood, and her followers petition her for war and fertility matters. She is celebrated at spring and harvest festivals, where women henna their hands, braid their hair, and wear the finest adornments in tribute. Many of her myths and attributes have been assimilated with Asherah and Astarte, and some scholars suggest Anath was merged with Astarte to form Atargatis. Anath is usually depicted nude, with flowers in her hands standing upon a lion, or as a young girl in battle gear.

Andraste: Celtic goddess of war. The mother of victory and combat, Andraste was evoked before battles to predict the outcome, and if necessary, alter it. She was called the Invincible One, and her name is translated as "She Who Has Not Fallen." In her light aspect, Andraste is a lunar deity, ruling over love and fertility. Her sacred animals are hares and ravens.

Angerona: Roman goddess of silence. A protective goddess of Rome, Angerona is the Secret-Keeper, guardian of the sacred name of the city. She is depicted with a bandaged mouth, one finger to her lips, demanding silence. She also rules fear and sorrow, driving these emotions away from the citizens of Rome. Her festival, the Angeronalia, is held on December 21st.

Anna Perenna: Roman goddess of time. Worshipped by both Etruscans and Romans, Anna Perenna is the moon goddess of the year. Her name translates as "She Who Lasts Many Years" or "Eternal Stream." She rules cycles of renewal and longevity, and the health of humans, plants, and animals. She supplies her people with abundance and plenty, and forests are her holy ground. In some myths and legends she is described as a young vibrant girl; in others she is an older woman. The personification of beginnings, endings, and memory, Anna Perenna's spring festival is celebrated on March 15th.

Annapatni: Hindu goddess of food and nourishment.

Antevorta: Prophecy goddess of Rome. The first aspect of the Camenae, Antevorta is a prophetic goddess whose name translates as "Before Change." Her powers rule the past as it turns toward the future, and are mainly invoked during the birth of a child. With her aspects Carmenta and Postvorta, Antevora is also a goddess of healing, poetry, and magickal charms.

Anuket: Egyptian goddess of the overflow. The personification of the annual flooding of the Nile River, Anuket is worshipped as an agricultural goddess. She nourishes the field and grains, bringing life, food, and prosperity to the land of Egypt. Her name means embracer, and her symbols are the cowrie shell, water jugs, the yoni, coins, and fish. As patroness of the poor, she supplies those in need with wealth and fertility. Anuket is generally depicted as a gazelle, or as a full-breasted woman with a reed-and-ostrich-feather headdress.

Apakura: Familial goddess of Polynesia. A mother goddess worshipped by the Maori of New Zealand, she has many children, and focuses on teaching her sons the path to excellence, wisdom, and victory. A serious-minded goddess, Apakura is the personification of home and family, and the strength and support one gains from close relations. In her dark aspect, Apakura is the Vengeful Mother, demanding her children avenge the wrongful death of their brother.

Apate: Greek goddess of deceit. The first to rise out of Pandora's jar, Apate is the spirit of manipulation, deception, trickery, and fraud. She is the daughter of Nyx and sister to Nemesis.

Aphrodite: Greek goddess of love and war. Daughter of the sea, Aphrodite is the goddess of beauty, love, and pleasure. Though she rules marriages and the love within them, she is also the goddess of illicit affairs. Thought to have originated from the Mesopotamian goddesses Astarte and Ishtar, Aphrodite has been associated with war and battles. She teaches dedication and love of the self, and is known for her quick and sometimes unscrupulous responses to petitions. Her symbols are the ocean, doves, apples, roses, and the mirror.

Arachne: Greek goddess of weaving. At some times considered as a priestess, others as a goddess, Arachne is described as a young woman who offended the goddess Athena by speaking the truth.

Skilled at the art of weaving, Arachne studied under Athena and is challenged by her to produce a tapestry. Arachne embroiders a scene that shows the gods of Olympus in an ill light. Outraged, Athena turns her into a spider. Arachne is the goddess of time, and of truth. She teaches her followers to speak the truth, and to weave honesty within their lives from a place of love and concern instead of pride and ego.

Ararat: Creation goddess of Turkey. Known throughout Turkey and Armenia, Ararat is embodied as the famous Mount Ararat, the land of mountains where the gods live. She is an earth goddess, creating life from her bones and sustaining it throughout all time. Her name means "a piece of creation," and she is invoked with soil and greenery.

Ardwinna: Celtic goddess of the forest. Identified with the Roman goddess Diana, Ardwinna is a woodland deity of the hunt. She supplies humanity with the meat of animals, and teaches respect for the forests and the life within them. She demands a tithe for any animal killed within her domain. Ardwinna is often depicted riding through the forest on a wild boar.

Arianrhod: Moon goddess of Wales. Arianrhod is the Mother aspect of the Triple Goddess, forming the triad with Blodeuwedd and Cerridwen. Her name means "silver disc," and she is called the Silver Wheel That Descends into the Sea. Known throughout Celtic regions, Arianrhod is able to shapeshift into an owl and rules the moon, the stars, and the sea. A goddess of prophecy and dreams, she offers a glimpse of both the future and the past to petitioners who come to her with an open heart and mind. As ruler of reincarnation, karma, and the magickal realms, Arianrhod receives the dead and guides them to the next stage of existence. She is a prime personification of authority and feminine power, and her role as timekeeper is represented by the Wheel of the Year. Arianrod is one of the five goddesses of Avalon, along with Blodeuwedd, Branwen, Cerridwen, and Rhiannon.

Arinna: Turkish goddess of the sun. Arinna is the principal goddess of the Hittite empire. She is seen as a warm, benevolent deity, offering protection from natural disasters, war, and illness. Consort of the weather god, she rules the power of the sun and the happiness it brings.

Armathr: Prosperity goddess of Iceland. Seen as the Goddess Incarnate, Armathr is represented as a sacred stone, which was revered by Icelandic peoples. She is the mother of prosperity, money, and business matters.

Arnamentia: Celtic goddess of flowing water. As the goddess of spiritual healing and purification, Arnamentia rules all bodies of water, including springs and rivers. In times of trouble and depression she offers renewal of the mind, body, and soul.

Artemis: Greek goddess of the hunt. Artemis is the Olympian goddess of the wilderness, and ruler of forests, woodlands, and wild animals. Also known as a goddess of childbirth, Artemis is the protector of young girls until they reach the age of marriage. As the Virgin Huntress, she is the personification of independence and self-reliance, and the defender of the weak and abused. Artemis is usually depicted as a young woman holding a bow and arrow. The deer, the bear, and the cypress tree are sacred to her.

Artimpaasa: Scythian goddess of the moon. Artimpaasa is the ruler of love, from familial relations to sensual pairings. She is worshipped as the moon, and the flow of the tides.

Artio: Celtic goddess of wildlife. As the goddess of the hunt, Artio rules woodlands, fertility, and wild animals. She carries the power of abundance, rejuvenating the fields after the harvest. Her name translates as "bear," and the female bear is sacred to her. Through this association, Artio is also seen as a shamanistic goddess, guiding her followers through the shadow side of existence in order to embrace the light.

Aryong Jong: Nourishing goddess of Korea. The people of Korea depend upon Aryong Jong to supply the earth with water. She allows the rains to fall and nourish crops, enabling the survival of civilization.

Asase Yaa: Harvest goddess of Africa. The Ashanti of West Africa refer to Asase Yaa as "Old Woman Earth." Farmers invoke her in the fields to bless their crops. She is the ultimate harvest, helping her children to sow the seeds they have planted throughout their lives. Asase Yaa is worshipped as the mother of humanity, supplying her children with life and embracing them once more upon death. She is the bending of the back, the sweat, the toil, and the ultimate reward of nourishment. Thursday is her sacred day.

Asherah: The great goddess of the Middle East. Known as the Queen of Gods and Ruler of Heaven, Asherah is usually depicted as a curly-haired goddess riding a sacred lion, holding flowers or serpents within her hands. Mentioned throughout the Old Testament, she was worshipped throughout ancient Israel as the consort of Yahweh, and is thought to have evolved into the goddess Shekina. Goddess of the sea, Asherah is the essence of divine wisdom and ultimate femininity. Her images were found carved into living trees, outside of homes, and on altar poles and walking staffs. Her symbols include the Tree of Life, lilies, and cows.

Ashiakle: African goddess of wealth. A West African deity, Ashiakle is worshipped throughout Ghana as a wealth and fertility goddess. She is the ruler of the sea and the treasures within.

Ashnan: Mesopotamian goddess of grain. Daughter of the Sumerian god Enlil, Ashnan is an agricultural and domestic goddess. She is the protector and nourisher of fertile lands, providing the people with grain and vegetation. Ahsnan's role is also to provide food and clothing to the gods of Mesopotamia. She is depicted as a maiden girl, with ears of corn sprouting from her shoulders.

Aspelenie: Eastern European goddess of hearth and home. Aspele-nie takes the form of a serpent, and was worshipped among pre-Christian Lithuanians. She is considered a servant of the sun goddess Saule, and is thought to bless the home with abundance and protection. The corners of a home and the area behind the stove are her sacred areas.

Astarte: Mesopotamian goddess of love and war. Similar to the goddess Ishtar, Astarte was worshipped throughout ancient Mesopotamia. Her name literally means "star," and she is the power behind the moon. The queen of both the morning and evening stars, she is the all-encompassing power over the heavens and all of creation. She rules the spirits of the dead, and is the mother of the astral bodies throughout the universe. As a love goddess, she rules passion, marriage, and sexual encounters, personifying the sensuality of a woman's body and the power of feminine independence. In her dark aspect she is the Warrior Queen, her passion channeled into war and battle victories. Her symbols include the sphinx, the dove, and the star.

Astghik: Armenian goddess of love. Astghik is the deity of beauty and love, ruling all bodies of water. She spreads love and fertility throughout Armenia by sprinkling rosewater on the land. Her festival is held in June, when celebrants release doves and sprinkle water on one another in her honor. She is offered roses by her petitioners.

Astraea: Justice goddess of Greece. An infinite virgin, Astraea is the goddess of justice. Originally, she is said to have lived among civilization but was later driven away by the disorder and chaos of humanity, and went to live among the stars. She represents the innocence and purity of the law-abiding.

Atargatis: Fertility goddess of Syria. Her role as mistress of the city and the Phoenician community ensured well-being throughout the trials and tribulations of everyday life. She is thought to be a merging of Anath and Astarte. Sometimes depicted as a woman wearing a crown and carrying grains, Atargatis is a goddess of fertility, giving her power and strength over nature. She is also seen as a mermaid goddess, ruling vegetation and moisture. She taught civilization religious and social structure, protected the people of her city, and provided inventions and ideas to aid humanity.

Athene: Greek goddess of wisdom. One of the three Greek virgin goddesses, Athene is the Wise Warrior, the personification of the autonomous female. Motherless, she rose fully formed from the head of Zeus, dressed in full battle armor. She is the protector of civilization, defending her city and people from enemies and teaching heroic endeavors. As the incarnation of wisdom and cunning intelligence, Athene is the philosopher, embodying reason and purity of thought. She is the patroness of weaving, metalworking, and weaponry. Often depicted with the goddess Nike at her side, her symbols are the owl and the olive tree. Athens is her city.

Atira: Native American goddess of the earth. The Pawnees of North America worshipped Atira as Earth Mother. Her people focused their efforts on hunting rather than farming, feeling that the act of agriculture and plowing was an insult to her. Atira is the Sacred Mother of all life, and her influence is most prevalent in untamed fields and forests.

Atthar: Arabic goddess of the sun. As the "Torch of the Gods," Atthar is the Mother of the pre-Islamic peoples of Arabia. She supplies light and strength, and is honored by the daily pouring of libations from high-standing altars and rooftops.

Auchimalgen: South American moon goddess. The Araucanians of Chile worshipped Auchimalgen as the moon, and as the spirit of compassion. She is considered the only goddess who cares for the human race, warding off evil and protecting humanity from despair and disaster. She is honored with silver bowls of water filled with white flowers.

Aurora: Roman goddess of the dawn. The personification of light and renewal, Aurora opens the gates of heaven so that her brother the sun can ride across the sky. She grants rejuvenation to her followers, washing away the deeds and misfortunes of the past. An amorous deity, Aurora has many mortal and immortal consorts, her bright sensuality and vibrancy making her difficult to resist. Her children are the four winds and the constellations.

Ausrine: Beauty goddess of eastern Europe. Lithuanians saw Ausrine as the morning star, or Venus. She is the daughter of Saule the sun goddess, and ruler of beauty, health, love, and youth. As Bringer of the Dawn, her beauty and light fill the world with magick and renewal, enchanting all who see her.

Axomama: Incan nourishment goddess. To the Inca of Peru, Axomama is the "Lady of Potatoes." An earth and agricultural deity, she supplies the people with food—potatoes being a main staple of their diet. She teaches cultivation and preservation.

Aziri: African goddess of prosperity. Aziri is the goddess of wealth and possessions, watching over marketplaces and business transactions. She distributes her material blessings and opportunities specifically to women, in an effort to maintain balance and avoid patriarchal reign and power. She is also seen as a goddess of love, protecting women from harmful pairings and from men who wish to marry for material gain. Thieves and swindlers, particularly those who abuse women, are subject to Aziri's great wrath.

Ba Ngu': Sea goddess of Indonesia. A kindhearted goddess, Ba Ngu' rescues sailors and fishermen who are stranded at sea. She is depicted as a dolphin, and when deceased dolphins are found washed up on shore, they are ritually buried in her honor.

Baba Yaga: Russian hag goddess. In Slavic countries, Baba Yaga is the ancient Witch, the Mistress of Magick who lives deep within the forests. Greatly feared and revered, she commands the spirits of the dead and is the keeper of wisdom. As the representation of the untameable, Baba Yaga is the guide to the shadow side of the self, teaching the lessons needed for growth and expansion. She is generally portrayed as an old, hag-like woman riding through the air on a mortar, the pestle used as an oar. She controls time and the elements, and she answers any question for those brave enough to ask.

Bachué: South American mother goddess. In Colombian mythology, Bachué is the primordial mother of humans and all of creation. Depicted as a large snake or dragon, she rose from Lake Iguaque with her mate to give birth to humanity. She taught the Colombian people the skills necessary for survival, and then returned to her home at the bottom of the lake.

Badb: Irish goddess of war. Often referred to as the Fury, Badb is the Crone aspect of the Triple Goddess, forming the triad with her sisters Macha and Morrigu. Mainly associated with death and destruction, she is also the keeper of the Sacred Cauldron, controlling fate, time, and rebirth. During warfare, she is known to shapeshift into a wolf or a crow, causing confusion among the warriors and manipulating the outcome of the battle.

Baduhenna: Scandinavian war goddess. Associated with woodlands, Baduhenna is a Frisian war goddess. In 28 AD, a battle between Frisian warriors and invading Roman soldiers took place in Baduhennawald, her sacred forest. The Frisians were victorious, and hundreds of Roman soldiers perished and were offered as a sacrifice to Baduhenna.

Banba, also *Banbha:* Irish goddess of protection. The poetic name of Ireland, Banba protects the land and its people from invaders. She forms a triad with her sisters Ériu and Fódla.

Banka-Mundi: Indian goddess of the hunt. Hindus worship Banka-Mundi for protection against the wild animals of the forests and jungles. Chanting her name is said to remove fear and to provide fertility.

Bardaichila: Storm goddess of India. The Assamese of northeastern India celebrate Bardaichila as the bringer of rains and winds. Her festival of dance and song is held in the spring.

Bast, also *Bastet:* Egyptian goddess of anointing. Goddess of the moon and the sunrise, Bast rules love, fertility, sensuality, and music. Her name translates as "Female of the Ointment Jar," and she is the creator of perfumes and oils. Bast is the mother of cats and the magickal power they contain, and is often depicted as a feline-headed woman holding a sistrum. As protector of women and children, she is the guardian of the household and the bringer of health and prosperity. Her main festival is held on October 31st, when worshippers celebrate with music, dancing, and lovemaking. She is thought to be the duality to Sekhmet.

Baubo, also *Iambe:* Greek goddess of laughter. When Demeter was wrung with depression over the abduction of Persephone, it was Baubo who lifted her spirits by performing a lewd song and dance. Baubo is the spirit of laughter, and represents the freedom from judgment in attaining joy and merriment. She is also the goddess of song, the measured meter of music, and the creator of iambic pentameter. Sexually liberated, and the mother of bawdy and scandalous humor, Baubo uses laughter and mirth to restore the soul.

Beiwe: Finnish spring goddess. The Sami people of Finland worshipped Beiwe as the goddess of spring and mental clarity. She is the power of the sun and fertility, enabling plants to grow and hence the survival of humanity. It is Beiwe who chases away the winter, and restores the sanity of those who have lost themselves during the darkness of the season. During her spring festival, her followers offer sacrifices of white animals, and cover their doorposts in butter to feed her. Beiwe's sacred animal is the reindeer.

Bellona: Etruscan goddess of war. Ancient Italians believed the goddess Bellona was the female counterpart of Mars, the god of war. She is depicted as a woman armed with a sword, spear, and torch, and she had her own temple in early Rome. In times of war and battle, Bellona is invoked for strategy and victory.

Bendis: Moon goddess of Thrace. Similar to Artemis, and at times identified with Hecate, Bendis is the deity of hunting, the moon, and the mysteries within the shadows. She is sexually independent, mating as she chooses, and is worshipped with orgies in wooded areas. She is the patroness of athletes and the physical body.

Benten, also **Benzaiten:** Japanese goddess of love. Depicted as a beautiful woman with eight arms riding a dragon, Benten is the ruler of love, music, and the arts. As a sea and water goddess, she is the purifying force that protects people from the darkness of the material world. Benten inspires the wise use of talents to their highest capabilities, and is the patroness of artists, dancers, musicians, and geishas. Provider of good luck and romance, her festival is celebrated at summer solstice in the many shrines still standing in Japan.

The Bereginy: Slavic nature goddesses. The Bereginy are the feminine spirits of nature and woodlands. They create magick in wild and untamed areas, and also promote fertility. They rule shorelines and have power over both earth and water.

Bia: Greek goddess of violent force. Bia is the spirit of the will, of energy and magickal strength. She is the winged companion of Zeus, and acts as the force and power of his avenging word. It is Bia who binds Prometheus for his crime against the gods of Olympus.

Biliku: Spider goddess of India. The people of the Andaman Islands of India worship Biliku as the Creatrix of the earth. She is a weather goddess who controls the sun and punishes offenders by bringing wind, storms, and monsoons. She weaves the webs of abundance and time, promising to supply her people with food and shelter for all eternity. However, Biliku's temper is harsh and unpredictable, and when she is slighted, she sends cyclonic storms to wash away houses and land. The Andamanese believe that the burning of wax incites Biliku's wrath, and they abstain from burning candles during the rainy season.

Bixia Yuanjin: Chinese goddess of birth. Bixia Yuanjin is of the Taoist tradition, and presides over the dawn, childbirth, and destiny. She is the bringer of light, banishing the darkness and instilling hope and wisdom. She sends messages to her followers in the clouds, and teaches the art of scrying. Bixia Yuanjin gives life to the mother's womb, as well as bestowing the karmic fate on the child.

Black Tara: Tibetan goddess of power. The goddess Tara is worshipped in many forms throughout Eurasia, and in the Hindu and Buddhist traditions. In her Black Tara manifestation, she controls the power of the will and measures our actions against our intentions. She administers the tests required for a soul to evolve and achieve enlightenment. The Black Tara rules over spirits and exorcisms, and heals afflictions of the mind and body.

Blodeuwedd: Welsh goddess of betrayal. Blodeuwedd, or "Flower Face," is the Maiden aspect of the Triple Goddess, forming the triad with Arianrhod and Cerridwen. Goddess of spring, initiations, and flowers, she is best known for the manipulation, adulterous betrayal, and murder of her husband Llew, or Lugh, the sun god. She is seen as the May queen, and her sacred marriage to Llew as the blood sacrifice needed in order for the Wheel of the Year to continue. As punishment for her betrayal, Blodeuwedd is turned into an owl, representing the inevitable evolution of the sensual maiden into the wise crone. She is considered to be a ninefold goddess unto herself for the nine blossoming flowers that created her: primrose, bean, broom, meadowsweet, burdock, nettle, oak, hawthorn, and chestnut. Blodeuwedd is one of the five goddesses of Avalon, along with Arianrhod, Branwen, Cerridwen, and Rhiannon.

Blue Tara: Tibetan goddess of liberation. The goddess Tara is worshipped in many forms throughout Eurasia, and in the Hindu and Buddhist traditions. In her Blue Tara manifestation, she liberates humanity from emotional obstacles as well as worldly boundaries. The Blue Tara is the protector, destroying the negative aspects of life in order to embrace the positive.

Boann: Irish goddess of poetry. Goddess of flowing waters, Boann is the goddess of spiritual insight and poetic prose. She inspires creativity by clearing the mind of debris and opening the soul to divine assistance. Boann rules all forms of poetry, as well as writing in general. Her presence is best invoked near running waters and riverbanks.

Bona Dea: Matron goddess of Rome. Roman women worshipped Bona Dea as a fertility goddess as well as the spirit of chastity. Her festivals on December 4th and May 1st were only accessible to women, and representations of men and beasts were forbidden inside her temple walls. Her powers of healing and restoration led the sick and disabled to be tended to in the gardens of her temples. Snakes are sacred to Bona Dea, and she was often invoked by slaves seeking freedom from bondage.

Brag-srin-mo: Tibetan ancestral goddess. The Demoness Mother of Creation, Brag-srin-mo used her abundant fertility and seduction skills to mate with the Monkey-Bodhisattva and bear six children. According to ancient myth, these children fed and multiplied, then shed their fur and tails, becoming the first people to walk the earth. *Brag-srin-mo* translates as "Ogress of the Cliff."

Branwen: Welsh goddess of beauty and love. One of the five goddesses of Avalon, Branwen translates as "White Raven" or "White Breasted." She is a Maiden goddess of sovereignty, springtime, and inspiration. The daughter of the sea, Branwen releases mistreated wives from bondage, and blesses them with a new beginning. She is the embodiment of vitality and freedom. Depicted as a beautiful young woman, Branwen is thought to be Venus, or the morning star. All birds and the waxing moon are her symbols.

Brigantia: Celtic goddess of summer. Often confused with Brigid, Brigantia is a solar goddess, ruling light and fire. She is the essence of the earth that holds all things in balance, promoting growth and fertility in all things. A healing goddess, her symbols include wells, springs, and serpents, and the chanting of her name is known to cure heinous diseases and wounds. Brigantia's festivals are Beltane and Midsummer, where she spreads the fires of creativity and inspiration among poets, artists, and musicians.

Brigid, or *Brigit, Brighid, Bride:* Irish goddess of the Sacred Flame. Brigid is a threefold goddess, each one her faces representing her dominion over poetry, healing, and smithcraft. Called the Great Goddess, she is keeper of the holy wells and rivers of healing and rebirth, as well as the sacred flames of creativity. Her festival Imbolc is celebrated on February 1st or 2nd, when sacred bonfires are kept burning all evening long to call forth the sun from hiding. Brigid is the mother of inventions and craftsmanship, the wise woman of healing, as well as the patroness of poets and priestesses. As Christian thought invaded the ancient world, the goddess Brigid was morphed into Saint Brigid of Kildare.

Britomartis: Virgin goddess of Crete. Goddess of the mountains, the seas, and hunting, Britomartis flows from Minoan into main Greek culture. She is the chaste maiden, avoiding advances from the lustful and the greedy. She blesses the hunter and the fisherman with tools and large bounties. Her symbols include fishing nets and lilies.

Brogla: Australian goddess of dance. The Aborigines of Australia depict Brogla as an attractive full-figured woman, naked and dancing. Her shaking hips and body control the weather and the winds. She is the sensual movement and flow of nature, and the patroness of dancers and choreographers.

Bugady Musun: Siberian mother of animals. Ruler of all life and food, Bugady Musun is the guardian of animals and all wildlife. Protector and guide to veterinarians, she is pictured as a very old but brawny woman. She is a shapeshifter, and will also appear to her petitioners as a reindeer or elk.

Bunzi: Central African goddess of rain. Daughter of Mboze, Bunzi is honored as the bringer of rain and the harvest. She is seen as a rainbow-colored snake, and she rewards her faithful worshippers with agricultural abundance.

Cailleach: Hag goddess of Scotland. The creator of mountains, hills, and valleys, Cailleach is the divine hag of Scottish Gaelic tradition. Builder of landscape and the wilderness, Cailleach carries a hammer or staff that freezes the ground during the three months of winter. She is the personification of winter, imprisoning spring and ruling the time between the last harvest and the beginning of spring. Her reign is ended by the arrival of Brigid and the sacred fires at Imbolc. The protector of wolves and deer, she is honored by hunters looking to feed on fresh meat during the darkness of the year. She is the bringer of nightmares, terrors, and eventually death. A great sorceress, healer, and midwife, Cailleach is pictured as a blue-faced crone, so near to death her face resembles a skeleton.

Caipora: Animal goddess of Brazil. Caipora is the Lady of Beasts in native South America. She lives within the forests and jungles, protecting animals from human hunters.

Calliope: Greek goddess of eloquence. The eldest of the nine Muses, Calliope is the essence of epic poetry. She empowers petitioners with grace of words and fluent expression. Her authority over poetic endeavors includes music, songwriting, and the confidence to perform.

Candelifera: Roman goddess of childbirth. Candelifera is the Candle Bearer, helping children emerge from the darkness of the womb into the light of the world. During labor and births, a candle is lit to invite her assistance and protection.

Canola: Irish goddess of music and dance. Canola fell asleep to the sound of the wind whispering along the bones of a gutted beached whale. Upon waking, she created the Irish harp, an instrument designed to capture the glorious sound she'd heard in her dreams. Patroness of musicians and bards, Canola aids inspiration and creativity.

Carmenta: Roman goddess of childbirth. One of the Camenae along with Antevorte and Postverta, Carmenta rules birth and prophecy. Her powers of divination pertain to the present, and she chants her prophecies in verse and song. Her name translates as "magickal spell," "oracle," or "charm," and she presides over poetry and bodies of water. As a goddess of contraception, Carmenta is invoked to guard against unwanted pregnancies. Honored primarily by women, her worship is said to predate the founding of Rome.

Carna: Goddess of physical health. Guardian of the human body and organs, Carna protects the life of humanity from spiritual attack and physical disease. She helps with the body's assimilation of food into energy, and teaches proper health for survival. Also the goddess of door hinges, Carna holds the separate worlds and dimensions together, as well as opening and closing doors and portals.

Ceres: Roman agriculture goddess. The goddess of grains, the harvest, and motherhood, Ceres is responsible for fertile soil and the nourishing earth. She taught humans to cultivate the land, and how to grow, conserve, and prepare food. Ceres is a compassionate and benign goddess, involving herself in the day-to-day life of her followers. Perhaps best known for her relentless pursuit of her kidnapped daughter Prosperpina, Ceres is the personification of a mother's love and dedication to her children. She is depicted carrying a scepter and a basket of fruits and flowers. Her Greek equivalent is Demeter.

Cerridwen: Welsh goddess of the cauldron. Keeper of the Sacred Cauldron, Cerridwen brews the magickal potions of divine wisdom and inspiration. She is the guardian of spiritual transformation, and the dispenser of righteous council and ultimate justice. Though she herself embodies the facets of Maiden, Mother, and Crone, Cerridwen is mainly honored in the Crone aspect, forming the triad with Blodeuwedd and Arianrhod. Goddess of the moon, Cerridwen rules the gifts of prophecy and magick, as well as the powers of death and rebirth. She is considered to be one of the five goddesses of Avalon. The white sow is her totem animal, and her sacred time frame for dedications and initiations is a year and a day.

Chalchiuhtlicue: Aztec goddess of water. Mother of lakes, streams, and the sea, Chalchiuhtlicue translates as "Jade Skirt" or "Lady Precious Green." She is a fertility deity, presiding over the birth of children and blessing them during their first bath. She is depicted dressed in clothing decorated with water lilies, holding a rattle in her hands. Chalchiuhtlicue's shrines and temples were built near streams and irrigation ditches, and she is mainly honored by those who make their living from water.

Ch'ang O: Chinese goddess of the moon. Ch'ang O and her husband were banished from heaven and forced to become mortal and live on the earth. Seeking to return to her place of glory, Ch'ang O took a full dose of an immortality pill meant for both her and her husband. She floated to the moon, destined to spend eternity alone. During the moon festival in China, women pray to Ch'ang

O to bring them their soul mate. Ch'ang O is offered sweet foods and incense, and the hare is her sacred animal.

Chantico: Aztec goddess of pleasure and pain. The goddess of hearth, home and volcanoes, Chantico blesses the home with wealth and stability. She rules over material abundance and precious things, protecting the home from thieves and loss. Chantico carries the balance of happiness and sorrow, pleasure and pain; she represents the duality of life, the earth, and people. Her femininity and sensual aspects, along with her association with pleasure and pain, has lead to her worship by those involved with BDSM sexual practices. She is depicted with a crown of cactus spikes and red serpents, and her name means "She Who Dwells in the House."

Chasca: Incan goddess of light. The Inca of Peru honored Chasca as the rising and setting sun. As goddess of dawn and twilight, she protects virgins and young girls from harm. She is considered a servant of the sun, and it is her light that enables flowers and plants to grow and thrive.

Chicomecoatl, also *Xilonen:* Aztec goddess of the earth. Chicomecoatl is the seven-snake maiden, the power behind the fertility of the earth and of humans. Honored as a goddess of food and drink, she is a nourishing deity, supplying her people with abundance and plenty. She is considered to be the female aspect of corn, and she is depicted in a red crown and garments, carrying ears of maize. Every September a young girl representing Chicomecoatl was sacrificed by the Aztec people in order to ensure Chicomecoatl's blessings. A Triple Goddess, Chicomecoatl is depicted as a young girl carrying flowers and fruits, a mother using the sun as protection, and an older woman carrying death in her touch.

Chihucoatl, also *Cihuacoatl:* Aztec goddess of childbirth. Often described as a large snake, Chihucoatl is the patroness of Aztec matrons. She rules labor, birth, midwives, and women who have died while giving birth. Chihucoatl is honored as an Earth

Mother, and her name translates as "Snake Woman." She helped create the human race, and her cry signaled a time of war or misery. Chihucoatl is depicted as young woman, or a hag with a skeletal face.

Chomo-Lung-Ma: Goddess mother of Tibet. The original name of Mount Everest, Chomo-Lung-Ma is said to live in the mountain, spreading her love and blessings over the world. She is the Great Mother of the Universe, providing wealth and spiritual insight to those who seek her counsel. Immoral behavior earns her wrath.

Chuang Mu: Chinese goddess of the boudoir. Chuang Mu is a love goddess, specifically presiding over sex, sensuality, and lust. Known as the Lady of the Bedchamber, she rules all activities of the bedroom, including sleep, dreams, and recovery from illness. She teaches the protocol of true lovemaking, and develops trust between partners. Traditionally dressed in red, Chuang Mu is honored with gifts of rice, tea, and fresh flowers during the annual Lantern Festival in China.

Chun T'i: Chinese goddess of war. Chun T'i is a sorceress, capable of providing miracles and magickal blessings. As the goddess of the dawn, she provides light to the earth and humanity, signifying clear thinking and clarity of desires. She protects against war, battles, and strife.

Chup Kamui: Chastity goddess of Japan. Chup Kamui was the moon goddess of the Ainu people, but after one night overlooking the earth and watching the sinful and amorous behavior of humanity, she begged her brother, the sun, to trade places with her. She became the sun, and he the moon. She is the symbol of modesty and innocence, and protects women from adulterous actions.

Circe: Greek goddess of sorcery. Best known for her role in the myth of Odysseus, Circe is the goddess of magick and spellcasting. She is attended by many priestesses, and specializes in illusions, transformations, and necromancy. She is the mother of magickal herbs and hallucinogens. Circe clears the mind and guides the lost and bewildered to their destinations, and her powers of seduction are based in the knowledge of positive feminine manipulation.

Coatlicue: Aztec goddess of life and death. Coatlicue, or "Serpent Skirt," is the mother of the gods in Aztec mythology. She is both nurturing and devouring, providing life from her womb and the horror of the grave from her heart. Her daughter Coyolxauhqui led Coatlicue's children in a rebellion against her, but her son Huitzilopochtli rose fully formed from her womb and slew his brothers and sisters. Coatlicue is depicted as a woman wearing a skirt made of snakes and a necklace of human hearts and bones, with claws for hands and feet.

Cocomama: Incan goddess of health and happiness. Cocomama was once a seductive and promiscuous woman with many lovers. When her suitors realized she was courting all of them, they banded together and murdered her, cutting her body in half. Her corpse then transformed into the first coca plant—the bush from which cocaine is extracted—and she became the goddess of health, joy, and pleasure. Incas believed chewing on the leaves of coca allowed men the ability to sexually please women, and brought wealth and happiness.

Copia: Roman goddess of abundance. Copia provides wealth and plenty to her followers. She is honored with wine and food, representing the overflowing fertility of the earth. She is depicted carrying a cornucopia filled with fruits, grains, and gold coins.

Corn Woman, **also** *Corn Maiden, Corn Mother, Yellow Woman:* Native American goddess of sustenance. Many Native Americans honor Corn Woman, the personification of maize and the fertility of the earth. She is a Triple Goddess as she grows from young to old, eventually sacrificing herself so that her body may nourish and seed the earth with corn, and the people may live and eat. Corn Woman teaches her followers how to properly pray and honor their deities, as well as how to sustain health through the cultivation of food.

Corra: Celtic goddess of prophecy. Mainly known throughout Scotland, Corra is a deity of magick and divination, blessing seekers with transcendental knowledge. She is known to shapeshift into the crane, a sacred bird associated with astral travel and spiritual knowledge.

Coventina: Celtic goddess of healing. Coventina is a river deity, and is associated with all running water. Her followers tossed coins and sacred objects into wells as an offering for her blessings. She is connected to healing and prophecy, and the ebb and flow of time and abundance. Her symbols are the cup, the cauldron, and all coins.

Coyolxauhqui: Aztec goddess of the moon. Daughter of Coatlicue, it is Coyolxauhqui who led her brothers and sisters to kill their mother. After her brother Huitzilopochtli decapitated her, her head was placed in the sky and formed the moon. Her name means "golden bells," and she is depicted with bells on her cheeks.

Creddylad, also *Cordelia:* Welsh goddess of spring. Creddylad is a beautiful maiden, dancing through fields with the faeries, her magick bringing life to the spring and summer flowers and vegetation. Often referred to as the May queen, she is a love goddess, fighting to protect the bonds of true love.

Cybele: Roman mother of the gods. Cybele is seen as a fertility and nature goddess, presiding over caves and mountaintops. She protects the city and its people from invaders and war. When her consort Attis was castrated and died of his wounds, she resurrected him. Her main followers were males who had ritually castrated themselves and assumed the roles and dress of women. Her priestess led her annual spring festival with music, dancing, drinking, and orgies.

Dana, also *Danu, Anu:* Earth-mother goddess of Ireland. Dana is the queen and mother of the Tuatha Dé Danann, a tribe of deities. Her name translates as "knowledge," and her influence spread throughout all Celtic lands. She is the power and magick of fertile soil, rivers, and vegetation. Dana is thought to be the Irish equivalent of the Welsh goddess Don.

Danu: Hindu goddess of water. Danu is the primordial force of water. She is the personification of the ocean, from which all creation in the universe springs. She produces streams and rivers to purify the earth, and bestows luck on those seeking treasure within her depths.

Demeter: Greek goddess of the harvest. Mother of agriculture and the seasonal year, Demeter is the goddess of the grains and parenthood. She taught humanity the process of sowing and ploughing to produce food. Sympathetic to suffering and grief, she always answers those who call for her aid. She is the Mother aspect of the Triple Goddess, forming the triad with Persephone and Hecate. Demeter's endurance and ferocity in the struggle to rescue her daughter Persephone from the underworld express a mother's protective love for child. The equivalent of the Roman goddess Ceres, Demeter is usually depicted carrying a cornucopia filled with fruits and grains.

Devi: The great goddess of India. Devi is the ultimate female force in Hinduism. Her name literally translates as "Goddess," and she is worshipped by thousands of names. She is the Mother of the Universe, and the ultimate balance of darkness and light. Devi is at the core of every Hindu goddess, who can all be viewed as manifestations of her. She is somewhat synonymous with Shakti.

Dewi Nawang Sasih: Rice goddess of Indonesia. The Sundanese people of Indonesia believe that Dewi Nawang Sasih gave them the gift of rice. She taught women the recipe to make one grain of rice reproduce into many, under the condition that no man was ever to touch a woman's cooking utensils. One man, who felt he was superior, disobeyed her and touched an implement. Angered, Dewi Nawang Sasih left the earth, taking with her the power of reproducing rice.

Diana: Roman queen of Witches. Diana is the independent huntress, the virgin of woodlands and forests, and guardian of all that is wild and free. A moon deity, she is known for her great beauty, magickal skills, and her protection of women who practice magickal arts. She is the keeper of wild and domesticated animals, and the patroness of slaves and the poor. Often depicted carrying a bow and arrow and surrounded by animals, Diana is quick to anger when slighted. Her annual festival is held on August 13th; she is said to protect the harvests from the coming storms. Artemis is the Greek equivalent of Diana.

Dike: Greek goddess of justice. One of the Horai, Dike is a springtime deity, bringing about the changing of the seasons. She rules human justice, fair judgments, customs, and cultural law. Dike bestows and teaches morality, and is one of the guardians of the gates of heaven. She is depicted as a winged woman carrying a torch.

Don: Welsh mother goddess. The equivalent of the Irish Dana, Don is an earth goddess and mother of the gods. She is the power of family and trust, and her powers of fertility nourish the soil as well as the waters of the earth. Her children, including her daughter Arianrhod, represent all that is light and good, and they battle against darkness and evil.

Druantia: Celtic queen of the Druids. Seen as the eternal wise and knowledgeable mother, Druantia is linked with oak trees and the Druids. She guides seekers to their true paths, instructing and teaching the sacred ways of the forest. She created the Celtic tree calendar and rules acts of passion, fertility, and sex. As queen of the dryads, Druantia protects trees and woodlands.

Dugnai: Eastern European goddess of the hearth. Dugnai is the patroness of kitchen Witches in Lithuania. She rules the hearth and home, and supplies families with fresh food. Herbal knowledge, magickal cooking, and baking all fall under her domain. She is honored with offerings of fresh bread and liquor.

Durga: Protection goddess of India. Durga is depicted with ten to eighteen arms, riding a tiger and carrying various weapons and sacred objects in her hands. She destroys the evil forces that attack humanity, such as jealousy, prejudice, and the ego, as well as the sinful nature of people. She possesses unlimited power and signifies the inevitable triumph of virtue over darkness. Durga is the Warrior Mother, and teaches her followers to receive the benefits of truth and love while protecting against the negative energies of the world.

Dziewanna, **also** *Devana, Diiwica:* Slavic goddess of the hunt. Similar to the Roman Diana, Dziewanna was worshipped throughout eastern Europe as the Maiden goddess of the forest. She is the bringer of spring, influencing agriculture and the weather, and is particularly celebrated by farmers. As a lunar goddess she is thought to run through the mountains with wild dogs or wolves during the three nights of the full moon. She is the infinite virgin, or rather, independent deity, having many mates but settling with none.

Dzydzilelya: Polish goddess of love. Ruler of love, marriage, and sexuality, Dzydzilelya is depicted throughout Slavic countries as a beautiful maiden full of passion. Similar to the Roman Venus, she is the Maiden goddess, embracing the roles of both chastity and seduction throughout her myths. As a fertility deity she blesses the womb of women in love.

Eir: Norse goddess of healing. She is a master physician, wielding power in the healing of the mind, body, and spirit; shamanic and energetic healings fall within her realm. Eir knows the secret powers of herbs, and bestows healing and wisdom to the women who seek her out. She is one of Frigg's twelve handmaidens, and is also counted among the Valkyries, using her talents to resurrect the dead. A patroness of those in health-related fields, Eir teaches women the secrets of the healing arts.

Eka Abassi: Goddess of the Ibibio people of Africa. She is the creator of life, coming before all existence and creating humans. Her consort and son is Obumo, the god of thunder and rain. It is said that Eka Abassi may not be spoken of among other gods, as she is so far beyond them all.

Elli : Norse giantess goddess of old age. Elli challenged and defeated Thor, the god of thunder, in a wrestling match, showing the cleverness and survival skill of one who has lived to old age. She is the embodiment of the Crone, the wisdom and strength of the elderly.

Enekpe: African goddess of family. Enekpe is the Guardian of Destiny, particularly within the familial blood line. It is said her worshippers went to war, and were threatened with extinction. Enekpe offered herself as a sacrifice in order to save her people. She was buried alive on the field of battle, and her tribe was saved, their linage blessed by her blood for eternity.

Eostre, also *Ostara:* Goddess of spring to the Saxon and Germanic tribes. Eostre is usually depicted as an adolescent girl or as a buxom young woman, representing the beginning of the spring season and the ripeness found within. Her name is derived from *eastre,* an ancient word for spring. The Christian holiday Easter is actually named for Eostre's festival, where she was honored as a fertility goddess with painted eggs and sweet foods.

Epona: Celtic-Saxon goddess of horses. Epona was revered throughout Gaul and Britain, her worship even spreading to Rome and a few Germanic tribes. As a protector of horses, livestock, and hounds, she is primarily worshipped by those whose livelihood depend upon these animals. Shrines were kept in stables and in homes, with whips, harnesses, or baskets of fruit symbolizing Epona. In ancient art, she is usually depicted sitting upon a throne surrounded by mares or hounds.

Erce: Anglo-Saxon goddess of the earth. Erce is known as "Earth as Lady," and is the female representation of the Wheel of the Year, or seasonal changes. She is worshipped as the Triple Goddess, and her name can be chanted as an invocation to the earth.

Ereshkigal: Sumerian goddess of the underworld. Ereshkigal was worshipped throughout the Mesopotamian region, her main following in Sumer and Babylon. She is the goddess of Irkalla, the underworld kingdom where the dead reside. Older sister and counterpart to Inanna/Ishtar, Ereshkigal represents the dark, the unseen, the shadow side of the soul. Only she can give laws, pass judgment, or hold any power in the underworld. Her consort is Nergal, and the story of their love is often praised in Mesopotamian hymns.

The Erinyes: Hag goddesses of Greece. The Erinyes are older than the Olympian gods. They are a trinity of Dark Crone goddesses who punish the wicked on earth as well as in the underworld. They are particularly aggressive against murderers and blasphemers, and often cause insanity in their victims. Their wrath can only be calmed by the persecuted seeking atonement. The Erinyes are Tisiphone the Avenger, Alecto the Unresting, and Megaera the Jealous. They are the Greek equivalent of the Roman Furies.

Ériu: Sovereign goddess of Ireland. Ériu is the daughter of the Dagda, High King of the Tuatha Dé Danann. She forms a triad with her sisters Banba and Fódla, and is considered to be the personification of Ireland.

Ertha: Germanic earth goddess. Ertha is a goddess of fertility, domestic life, and is considered to be the matron of kitchen

Witches. She is celebrated at each season change, with smoke from the burning of fir boughs invoking her presence. Evergreens are sacred to her.

Erua, also *Zarpanitu:* Babylonian goddess of birth. Erua rules over the marriages and births of all creatures within her lands. She was celebrated annually in Babylon at the new year. Consort of Marduk, Erua can also be an alternate title for Inanna or Ishtar.

Erzulie: West African goddess of love. Originally a goddess of Africa, Erzulie is now mainly worshipped in the Voudun cultures of the Afro-Carribean. She is a goddess of beauty, prosperity, and the performing arts—especially dance. She is feared and loved for her tremendous power, and known for her severe mood swings. Followers of Erzulie say once you are in her favor, you will never want again; cross her, and your remaining days will be spent suffering in her wrath. Erzulie is the patroness of prostitutes and all sexual behavior. She is typically invoked with ceremonial dance, or ritual baths filled with expensive oils and perfumes.

Estsanatlehi, also *Changing Woman, Turquoise Woman, White Shell Woman:* Native American goddess of succession. Estsanatlehi, or "Self-Renewing One," is known among the Navajo and Apache peoples. She is able to make herself young whenever she begins to age. She is of the earth, born of darkness and dawn, creating people from dust and the skin of her breasts and nipples. Estsanatlehi is a cyclical goddess, a representation of the changing seasons of the earth and humanity. She is depicted as an attractive Native American woman, anywhere from age twelve to eighty; her symbols are hoops, rainbows, and mountains.

Etugen, also *Itugen:* Mongolian earth goddess. The virginal Etugen is a fertility goddess, ruler of grasses and animals. Her name comes from Otuken, the holy mountain, and female shamans in Siberia were often named for her. Trees are a symbol of her nurturing spirit.

Euphrosyne: Greek goddess of mirth. One of the Three Graces, Euphrosyne is the goddess of good cheer, joy, laughter, and merriment. She forms a triad with her sisters Aglaia and Thalia.

Eurynome: Great goddess of the Greeks. Creatrix of all things, Eurynome was born of the chaos before the world. She is the mother of all pleasure. She danced and separated water from sky, and light from darkness. From the wind she molded a lover, the snake Ophion; she mated with him and gave birth to the Universal Egg, from which land, plants, and animals sprung. Eventually, Ophion began to boast that he was the creator of all things; Eurynome kicked out his teeth and cast him out of heaven.

Evaki: South American goddess of sleep. For the Bakairi Indians of Brazil, Evaki is the ruler of night and day. She stole sleep from the lizards and shared it with all living things. It is she who teaches the power of dreams and their meanings. Guardian of the sun, Evaki keeps the light in a jar, releasing it each morning and recapturing it at night.

Faumea: Ocean goddess of Polynesia. Faumea is a fertility and sensuality goddess, as well as deity of protection and personal boundaries. She rules the ocean with her consort, Tangaroa, and together they control the sea life and the creatures of air. Faumea's vagina is filled with man-eating eels, shielding her from unwanted advances; she taught her husband how to safely entice them out.

Feronia: Roman goddess of the harvest. Woodlands, rivers, and springs are sacred to Feronia. She is the guardian of all things wild and fertile, and ensures bountiful harvests to all who honor her. She protects travelers and slaves who seek freedom. Her festival is celebrated on November 15th, when she was offered fresh fruits and grains.

Flidais: Irish goddess of the woodlands. Flidais rides through the forests in a chariot pulled by deer. She is a deity with great sexual power, seducing powerful male mortals. She is a fertility goddess with many children, and supplies abundance and nourishment with her cow that gives milk to three hundred people. She is depicted with long, luxurious hair.

Flora: Spring goddess of Rome. As the goddess of flowers and springtime, Flora is celebrated throughout April and early May with dancing, singing, and drinking. She rules flowering plants and fruits, and protects vegetation from disease and rot. She is considered to be a handmaiden of Ceres and rules the blossoming of plants, and girls into womanhood.

Fódla: Sovereign goddess of Ireland. Fódla forms a triad with her sisters Banba and Ériu. She is associated with agriculture, and is the force behind the green, rolling hills of the land.

Fortuna: Roman goddess of fortune. Fortuna was worshipped in many shrines throughout ancient Rome. She is the personification of luck, whether good or bad, and also rules fate, fortune, and divination. Her presence has a positive effect on all areas of life, and she blesses gardens and couples in love with fertility. Fortuna is the patroness of the bath house, and she is often depicted as blind and veiled.

Fravashi: Persian spirit guide. Fravashi translates as "She Who Is Many." She was created from the souls of all living creatures, including those yet to be born upon the earth. She helps guide the soul in decision making, and is often thought of as the epitome of intuition and the divinity of humanity. Fravashi is pure love, and also teaches the benefits of sacred pleasure.

Freya: Norse goddess of love and war. Freya is the maiden mistress, and described as the most beautiful of all goddesses. No male mortal or god can resist her. She is invoked for happiness in love and familial relations, as well as with sex and sensuality issues. As the Queen of the Valkyries, she gathers the souls of the dead and slain warriors and escorts them to the afterlife. Freya is the mistress of cats, and is thought to have inspired all poetry. Her sacred day is Friday, and her number thirteen.

Frigga: Norse mother goddess. Frigga is the deity of marriage and household order, including the domestic arts. She is the patroness of matrons, and provides protection to women and children. Frigga is a seer who observes all dimensions of existence, and has the power of divination and prophecy; however, she does not tell what she knows. As the wife of Odin, she rules the gods.

Gaia: Earth goddess of Greece. Gaia is the primordial mother of the gods, and all creation sprang from her union with the sky. She is the embodiment of the earth and land, carrying the sea and mountains upon her breast. She is represented by all things green and lush, and is depicted as a full-figured woman rising from fertile soil.

Gbadu: West African goddess of fate. Gbadu is a compassionate goddess, using her power to halt the chaos that reigns on earth. Honored by the Fon, or Dahomey people of Benin, she teaches divination and oracular work.

Gleti: West African moon goddess. To the Fon people, Gleti is the mother of the stars and planets, and is married to the sun god. She rules light and love, and it is said that eclipses are the result of Gleti mating with her husband.

Green Tara: Tibetan goddess of compassion. The goddess Tara is worshipped in many forms throughout Eurasia, and in the Hindu and Buddhist traditions. The Green Tara is the mother of compassion, and guards against natural disasters. She spiritually nurtures humanity, relieving suffering and misery in relation to worldly affairs. The Green Tara teaches self-mastery through meditation and diligent work.

Gula: Mesopotamian goddess of healing. As the patroness of physicians, Gula is the mother of healing the body, mind, and soul. After the Great Flood, it is Gula who restores life to humanity.

She is also a goddess of retribution, poisoning and visiting illness on all wrongdoers. She rules all herbs and incantations used for health-related issues. Her sacred animal is the dog.

Gullveig, **also** *Heid:* Golden goddess of Scandinavia. A great sorceress with the gift of sight and a love for gold, Gullveig is associated with fertility, prosperity, reincarnation, and rebirth. She was burned at the stake three times in Odin's hall, and all three times she stepped from the flames unscathed. She is represented by any golden object.

Gunnlod: Norse goddess of poetry. A giantess, Gunnlod is the keeper of Odrerir, the mead of poetry. The brew was contained in three cauldrons hidden in the depths of the earth, represented by the womb of Gunnlod. Odin seduced her for three days and three nights and stole the mead—i.e., her virginity. Gunnlod's mead, or wise blood, contained the powers of immortality and magick, and transformed Odin into a supreme god.

Gyhldeptis: Forest goddess of Native America. Gyhldeptis, or "Lady Hanging Hair," is honored by the Tlingit and Haida peoples of northwest America. She is the protector of people and of the gods, and is the spirit of the trees, usually represented by cedarwood branches. When a whirlpool threatened the destruction of her people, Gyhldeptis called forth all the elements and synthesized them into one energy to work within her. She then transformed the whirlpool into a river, nourishing the land and humanity.

Habondia: Germanic earth goddess. Throughout northern Europe, Habondia was worshipped as a harvest deity, granting abundance and prosperity to fields, crops, and herds. Infinitely generous, she promotes growth in all areas of life.

Haltia, **also** *Haltija:* Finnish goddess of hearth and home. Haltia brings good luck and health to those who invite her into their home; she resides in a roof beam in the homes of her devotees.

When a Baltic Finn family changed residences, the family took the beam with them to ensure Haltia's continued blessings.

Hathor: Egyptian goddess of love and music. The embodiment of success and abundance, Hathor rules all aspects of beauty, wealth, and the arts. She is the patroness of dancers and musicians, and rules all aspects of womanhood and femininity. A benign deity, Hathor bestows happiness and joy on her followers, and is most often worshipped with fragrant perfumes, songs, and dance rituals. She is depicted as a beautiful woman with the ears of a cow, carrying a sistrum. Her traditional offerings are two mirrors and myrrh.

Haumea: Hawaiian mother goddess. Haumea is symbolized by the supernatural Makalei tree, which bears coconut, bamboo, and sugarcane, and also attracts fish when its branches are dipped into the ocean. She is an abundance goddess, ensuring her children are forever supplied and nourished with food. As the sacred mother, Haumea gives birth to the Hawaiian gods from different body parts, including Pele and Hi'iaka. Her breast milk forms the rivers of the earth, and she eternally evolves from Maiden to Crone, symbolizing the cycle of life and of the earth.

Hebat, also *Kheba, Khepat:* Matron goddess of Mesopotamia. The ancient Hurrians worshipped Hebat as the consort of the storm god Teshub. She controls the power and light of the sun, and protects women during times of war. The incarnation of royalty and beauty, Hebat is depicted as a domesticated woman, either seated on a throne or standing on a lion.

Hecate: Witch goddess of Greece. Hecate is the Crone aspect of the Triple Goddess, forming the triad with Persephone and Demeter; although she also appears as having three faces unto herself. She has power over heaven, earth, and the underworld, and is often referred to as the "Queen of Ghosts." As the guardian of the spiritworld, she protects ghosts from harm and from causing mischief. Originally a goddess of the wilderness and childbirth, Hecate is most often associated with the crossroads—a place of spiritual wisdom and dark intuitive magick. The ultimate sorceress and diviner, Hecate teaches her followers the path of the Witch, and guides the seeker to the depths of the unconscious mind.

Heimarmene: Greek goddess of fate. Heimarmene rules astrology and astrological fate. She is the force of the inevitable in every living thing, and the power that keeps the order of the universe.

Hekit, also *Heqet, Hepat:* Egyptian goddess of midwives. Hekit is portrayed as a frog sitting on a lotus, or as a woman with a frog's head. She is the force of life and fertility, and the goddess of the last stages of birth, breathing life into the child's body. She is the patroness of midwives and nurses, and her amulet is worn by women in labor to protect them from pain and death.

Hel: Norse goddess of the underworld. Hel controls the souls of the wicked, and those who die of sickness or old age in her underworld kingdom of Helheim. She is the dark hag who walks the line between life and death, and thins the veil between the worlds. It is Hel who gifts Odin with his twin ravens of prophecy and wisdom. The patroness of Nordic shamans, Hel is depicted as half alive and half dead, her lower body the rotting flesh of a corpse, and her face and torso a living woman.

Hera: Greek queen of heaven. Hera is the Olympian queen of gods, and the goddess of the sky, marriage, and women. She is the guide for every part of a woman's life, including love and financial independence. She despises betrayal, particularly within the union of marriage, and her methods of retribution are harsh. *Hera* translates as "Great Lady," and her symbols are the peacock, the cuckoo bird, and pomegranates.

Hestia: Greek goddess of hearth and home. Hestia embodies both the Maiden and the Crone, as she is the first child of Kronos but the last to be freed from his belly by Zeus. As the goddess of the sacred flame, Hestia is worshipped in the home, where she provides protection and the warmth needed to sustain life. It is her presence within the home that produces security, blessings, and familial love. Hestia is a true virgin goddess, constantly fending off sexual advances from both mortals and gods, choosing instead to remain pure. She is depicted either as a young woman wearing a veil or as an older, matronly figure.

Hi'iaka: Hawaiian resurrection goddess. Daughter of Haumea and sister of Pele, Hi'iaka is the personification of Hawaii, and rules the hills, cliffs, and caves. She is creator of dance and the patroness of hula dancers. When Pele repeatedly kills her lover, Hi'iaka resurrects him each time, refusing to surrender him or the love they share. Hi'iaka was born from the cosmic egg produced from Haumea's mouth and kept warm in Pele's bosom. A joyful goddess, she is honored with dance and song.

Hina: Great goddess of Hawaii. Hina is a many-faced goddess who lives in the moon and travels by following the path of rainbows. Her two heads symbolize day and night, as well as the light and the shadow side of the human soul. Hina is known as the Butterfly Goddess, carrying spiritual messages and creative ideas to her followers. She brings forth renewal from death, and creates positive communication between men and women. She is known by many names and aspects throughout Polynesian culture.

Hine: Great goddess of New Zealand. Hine can be viewed as the darker face of Hina, and is also considered a goddess unto herself in New Zealand culture. Hine is seen as the ancestor goddess from which all life emerges, and returns to upon death. Specifically, she is the ruler of night and the underworld, and in other aspects she rules arts and crafts.

Holda: Winter goddess of northern Europe. Holda is also known by the titles "Snow Queen" and "Mother Holle." She is mainly associated with the winter season, and is thought to bring prosperity to the kindhearted, and to punish the weak and lazy. Children were frightened into good behavior with tales of Holda coming to kidnap or beat them. Holda is also a goddess of nature, controlling snowfall and fog. She is depicted as a beautiful woman wearing red and white, and at Yuletide it is said she rides the wind to carry good fortune and health to those who honor her.

Hsi Wang Mu: Chinese goddess of immortality. Known as the "Queen Mother of the West," Hsi Wang Mu is the highest goddess in the Taoist pantheon. She is the embodiment of the yin principle, and she guides and protects spiritual women, granting them the power of prophetic dreams and visions. She is the goddess of life and death, and the guardian of the enchanted peaches that have the power of eternal life. Jade and pearls are sacred to her, and she is usually pictured surrounded by peacocks, cranes, and the phoenix.

Ilmatar, **also** *Luonnotar:* Finnish goddess of creation. Ilmatar created the world from three duck eggs, which hatched and brought forth the earth, the sky, and agriculture. When the yolks of the eggs combined to form the sun, Ilmatar called forth fresh spring water and planted seeds so that the earth would flourish. She is referred to as the Daughter of Nature.

Inanna: Sumerian goddess of love and war. Known as Ishtar by the Babylonians, Inanna was worshipped throughout Mesopotamia as the Queen of Heaven and Earth. She is a lunar goddess, and is seen as the morning and evening stars. Her powers of seduction and sensuality made her name synonymous with fertility and mating rituals. Sister of Ereshkigal, Inanna empowers the light side of the soul, imparting wisdom and the magick of life and death. As a war goddess, she protected her city and followers, dispensing justice and the laws of the land. Her symbols are the lion and the eight-pointed star.

Inari: Japanese goddess of nourishment. Inari is depicted in both male and female form. As a goddess, she is seen as a young woman with long, flowing hair; as a god, Inari is represented by an old man with a beard. She is the goddess of rice, and the patroness of farmers and merchants. She bestows prosperity and abundance on all who honor her.

Indrani: Hindu goddess of insight. Indrani is a goddess of great beauty, and is the wife and consort of the god Indra. She has one thousand eyes, and is usually depicted with a thunderbolt in one hand and a child in the other. She is all-seeing, and capable of perceiving the secrets of the material and the spiritual worlds. Elephants and lions are sacred to her.

Indunn: Norse goddess of youth. In Scandinavia, Indunn is the goddess of immortality, keeper of the magickal apples that offer eternal youth. She is the maiden patroness of springtime, and it is she who supplies the gods with everlasting life. Also a healer, Indunn strengthens the life force of the weak and sickly.

Inkosazana: African goddess of agriculture. The Zulu people call Inkosazana "Lady Heaven," as she rules the celestial bodies and the lives of women. She is the force that allows corn and other foodstuffs to grow. She is often associated with rainbows and rainfall.

Iris: Greek goddess of the rainbow. Iris is the messenger of the gods, and maidservant to Hera. She has power over the sea and the sky, and she is considered to be the bridge between heaven and earth, linking the gods to humanity. She is portrayed as a young woman with golden wings standing at the side of either Hera or Zeus.

Ishtar: Babylonian goddess of love and war. The equivalent of Inanna, Ishtar is mainly associated with sexual love and royalty. Her priestesses are believed to have been sacred courtesans found within the temples of the Goddess. Ishtar's power is greatest during the full moon, when she envelops lovers in fertile energy. Her role as protector and war goddess is due to her volatile temper, and her desire to right wrongs against women and her city.

Isis, also *Auset:* Goddess queen of Egypt. Goddess of magick and healing, Isis is the most well-known deity of the Egyptian pantheon. She is the patroness of women and children, and the honored protector of marriage and vows of love. The ultimate wife and mother, Isis uses her wisdom and sorcery to strengthen ancestral bonds, manifest change, and transform the world. The lotus flower and the sycamore tree are sacred to her.

Ista Devata: Goddess of individuality in India. Ista Devata is the patroness of the self found through enlightenment. She is the personification of the feminine Godhead found within each living soul. She teaches the power of transformation and transmutation as a way of understanding personal energy.

Itzpapalotl: Aztec goddess of seasons. Also known as "Obsidian Knife Butterfly," Itzpapalotl is the Dark Mother of creation and change. She controls the seasons of the year and agriculture, her fierce nature manifesting in droughts, storms, and death. Though she offers humans release from suffering and pain, it is a freedom that she can only supply through death. Itzpapalotl is depicted as a beautiful woman, or as a skeleton with butterfly wings embedded with blades.

Ix Chel: Mayan moon goddess. Ix Chel is the mother of the Mayan deities, and rules the cycles of life and death. She is the keeper of souls, and constantly evolves from a young woman into the wise crone. Mayan women were expected to complete a pilgrimage to Ix Chel's sacred island to offer the goddess gifts and receive her blessings. The guardian of weavers, artists, and musicians, Ix Chel offers her creative inspiration to all who seek her.

Ixtab: Mayan goddess of suicide. In Mayan society, suicide was an acceptable way to die, and would lead to the paradise of the afterlife. Ixtab is the guardian of those who killed themselves by hanging, as well as the keeper of souls of warriors and women who died in childbirth. She guides the souls to heaven and cares for them. In her seductress role, Ixtab mated with young, mortal men who, after sampling her, would go insane and pine after her affection forever. She is depicted as a dead and decomposing woman with a rope around her neck.

Izanami: Japanese goddess of life and death. Izanami is the goddess of the earth and of fertile soil, which gave birth to all gods and goddesses. She and her mate, Izangi, descended from heaven to create the earth. When Izanami gave birth to the god of fire, he burned Izanami to death, transforming her into an unsightly old woman. No longer fit for the natural world, Izanami traveled to the underworld and reigned as the goddess of death.

Jord: Norse goddess of the earth. Jord is the goddess of the wilderness and uncivilized areas of land. She is the mistress of Odin and the mother of Thor. A giantess, Jord is the personification of earth and the giver of life.

Julunggul: Australian goddess of initiation. The great goddess of Aborigines in northern Australia, Julunggul rules rites of passage and initiations. She guides young boys into manhood, giving them the strength and wisdom to overcome the trials of puberty. She is depicted as the rainbow serpent, holding powers of rebirth and immortality. A water goddess, Julunggul flows into people's lives, providing sacred dreams and the experiences needed for positive growth.

Juno: Roman mother of the gods. The equivalent of the Greek Hera, Juno is the protector of Rome and queen of the gods. She rules femininity in all its forms, guarding and guiding young girls into adulthood. As the patroness of marriage, Juno blesses her followers with the perfect mate, at the perfect time. Her sacred animal is the peacock, and the month of June is named for her.

Kali Ma: Hindu goddess of time. Kali Ma is the manifestation of the Divine Mother in Hindu society. She is most often depicted in her destroyer aspect, with black skin, a skirt of human limbs, and a necklace of skulls. She is the creating force of the universe, and is the eternal power of time, order, and chaos. She is dark and formless, and her unlimited power of transformation is often compared to the black holes found in outer space. She destroys that which is no longer needed, creating a void in which all things are possible. Kali Ma is the Shakti of Shiva, and also rules wild, untamed feminine strength.

Kamrusepas: Hittite healing goddess. Known as "The Mother," Kamrusepas is a powerful healer and sorceress, providing miracle healings and cures to the people of Mesopotamia. She is also a fertility and agricultural goddess, healing the land and plants from drought and neglect. She is a calm, benevolent force, appeasing anger and self-loathing. Honey and fruits are sacred to Kamrusepas.

Kamui Fuchi: Hearth goddess of Japan. Kamui Fuchi is the ancestress and tribal mother of the Ainu people of Japan. She guards the gateway between the natural world and the spirit world as the fire of the hearth, and demands that the fire never be completely extinguished. As the "Lady of the Home," she protects against evil spirits when offered rice, mugwort, and beer by her petitioners.

Kikimora: Slavic goddess of the home. A domestic goddess in eastern Europe, Kikimora rules all aspects of housekeeping and cooking. She provides blessings to those who are meticulous homemakers, but punishes the lazy with household chaos. She is also known as a deity of dreams and nightmares, and is said to appear spinning and weaving when a member of the household is set to die. Kikimora is depicted as an average woman with the legs and feet of a chicken.

Kipu-Tytto: Finnish goddess of suffering. Kipu-Tytto translates as "Pain Girl," and she resides in the underworld. The goddess of illness, death, and tragedy, she sings the ailing to their death and guides them to the next world. Kipu-Tytto is seen as a young woman with a black, pockmarked face or as an old, sickly crone.

Koevasi: Creatrix goddess of Melanesia. Koevasi is a Polynesian serpent goddess, ruling all aspects of creation, transformation, and rebirth. She is both the Mother and the Crone, the light and the dark of the universe.

Koliada, also *Koljada, Colleda:* Serbian goddess of time. Throughout eastern Europe, Koliada is celebrated as the winter solstice and the personification of time. She is the darkness that guides the spirit to the light, and a festival is held in her honor during Yuletide.

Krtya: Witch goddess of India. Krtya is the feminine state of enlightenment. She is the ultimate shapeshifter, having the ability to assume any form. She speaks the words of power, which can call anything into manifestation.

Kuan Yin, also *Quan Yin:* Chinese goddess of mercy. Worshipped throughout the world, Kuan Yin is the mother of compassion. Her name translates as "She Who Hears the Weeping World," and she accepts and responds to all prayers. Kuan Yin cares for the souls of the deceased, and relieves sinners from purgatory. As the patroness of healers, Kuan Yin cures ailments of mind, body, and spirit. Though she is sometimes depicted as a male deity, Kuan Yin is usually seen as an attractive woman carrying a jug of healing water; at times she is pictured as a figure with many arms and eleven heads.

Kunapipi, also *Gunapipi:* Australian goddess of puberty. To the aboriginal people, Kunapipi is a mother goddess, and protector of the brave and heroic. She gave birth to humanity, animals, and plants. It is said she swallows young boys, then regurgitates them into adulthood. Her totem is the rainbow serpent.

Kupala: Slavic goddess of herbs. In eastern Europe, Kupala is seen as a goddess of water and fire. She controls their magickal properties and rules all the plants of the earth. Kupala teaches the proper magickal uses of vegetation in spellcasting and rituals. Her sacred plant is the fern.

Lada: Eastern European goddess of spring. Lada is honored as a deity of springtime and love throughout Russia, Lithuania, and Poland. She is the May queen, consorting with her brother Lado to bring fertility and growth to the land. Lada creates harmony within the household and in marriages as she blesses unions of love with peace and goodwill. She is the mistress of flowers, and is described as a young lady wearing white and a flower-wreath crown.

Lady of Beasts: Animal goddess of the Middle East. The title "Lady of Beasts" is used to describe a variety of goddesses in many cultures. She is best known in the Middle East, stretching into Mesopotamia and the Indus Valley. She is the life-giving force of the universe, ruling wild forests, jungles, and the animals within them. A birth and fertility goddess, her presence is said to bless the reproduction of all women and animals. Lady of Beasts is generally depicted as a pregnant woman surrounded by untamed animals.

Lajja Gauri, also *Aditi:* Hindu goddess of the sky. Her name means "free," "unbound," or "limitless." Ancient art throughout India shows Lajja Gauri as a lotus-headed goddess, naked and adorned with jewels, her legs raised in a birthing or sexual position, exposing her vulva. She is the Infinite Mother, ruler over the conscious and unconscious minds, the past and the future, and the universe. The ultimate protector, she provides her children with safety, spiritual enlightenment, and material wealth; she also grants her worshippers an easy path to their heart's desire. Lajja Gauri is mentioned in the sacred Vedic texts as the Mother of All Gods, and the mediator between the mortals and the Divine.

Lakshmi: Hindu goddess of prosperity. Lakshmi is the epitome of wealth and abundance in both the material and spiritual realms. She rules prosperity in all it forms, and widely bestows her gifts on those who are open to receive. Celebrations of Lakshmi are held during the month of October. She is generally pictured wearing red and gold, standing on a blooming lotus with gold coins pouring from her hands. Full moons are sacred to her.

Lama: Intercession goddess of Mesopotamia. The Sumerians prayed to Lama for personal protection and advancement. She is the guardian of palaces and temples, carrying messages between the gods and humanity. Lama acts on behalf of the greater good, regardless of society's ideals of morality. She is seen as a woman in a long, tiered skirt.

Lamia: Greek serpent goddess. Lamia is originally a goddess of Libya, and quite possibly an extension of the goddess Lilith, but the most prevalent myths of Lamia come from her Greek assimilation. When Hera stole Lamia's children and destroyed them, Lamia went insane with grief, and transformed into an immortal demoness who hunted humans and drank the blood of children. She is a powerful sorceress and seductress, and is pictured as a serpent with a woman's head and torso.

Leshachikha: Slavic goddess of the forest. Leshachikha is seen in eastern Europe as a temperamental forest deity. She guards the land and animals of the wood, and punishes those who abuse them.

Leto: Greek goddess of motherhood. Mother of Artemis and Apollo, Leto protects the young and aids women suffering through difficult births. She is compassionate and kind to both humans and gods, and is said to answer all petitions made to her.

Lilith, also *Lilit:* Sumerian goddess of the wind. Lilith is thought to be the original Queen of Heaven in Sumer. Over time Lilith's qualities were integrated with Inanna's, and she became the handmaiden and constant companion of Inanna. She rules elemental air, wind, and storms, and seduces men into the temples for sexual rites. When the Hebrew traditions began to spread throughout the Middle East, Lilith was morphed into the first wife of Adam and merged with tales of Witches and demons to explain her dominant nature. In Sumer, Lilith was depicted as a full-figured woman with the wings and claws of a bird; she was later represented as half woman, half serpent by the Hebrews. Her symbols are the screech owl and the dark moon.

Lofn: Norse goddess of forbidden love. Lofn removes obstacles blocking true love, and happiness in marriage. She has a hedonistic nature, particularly in sexual manners, and rules adultery and forbidden liaisons.

Lucina: Roman goddess of light. Lucina is a deity of childbirth, guiding newborns into the light of the world. She protects women in labor, and is considered an aspect of Juno.

Lupa: Wolf goddess of Rome. Nursemaid and adoptive mother of Romulus and Remus, Lupa is the personification of fertility. She is the fierce protectiveness a mother has for her children. Her festival was celebrated with orgiastic rituals and the sacrifice of goats and dogs. Milk is sacred to her.

Ma Gu, also *Ma Ku:* Chinese goddess of longevity. Ma Gu translates as "Hemp Maid" or "Hemp Priestess." She is worshipped by the ritual smoking and spiritual use of cannabis in some modern Taoist traditions. She is the immortal protector of women and the deity of springtime, associating her with rebirth and fertility. Ma Gu breathes life into the world, has alchemical knowledge, and is depicted as an attractive woman with long fingernails.

Ma'at: Egyptian goddess of justice. Ma'at is the personification of divine order, truth, and moral law. She enforces traditions and customs, and annihilates chaos. Ma'at measures the heart of the dead against her feather of truth. If she finds the soul to be righteous, the deceased travels to the land of the dead; if not, the soul is destroyed. She is all powerful, as even the gods must abide by her laws and judgments.

Macha: War goddess of Ireland. Macha and her sisters Morrigu and Badb form a triad of war goddesses, ruling battles in Ireland. She is a seer, foretelling the deaths of warriors in battle as well as the outcomes of war. Macha is associated with land and horses. Crows are her totem.

Madre Vieja: Otomi goddess of creation. Madre Vieja, "Old Mother," is known throughout Mesoamerica as the creator of the universe. She rules the earth and the moon, and she created agriculture.

Mahuika: Maori goddess of fire. Mahuika lives in the underworld, and rules fire and earthquakes. She has flames for fingernails and toenails, and was tricked into giving fire to humanity. She is associated with caves and is responsible for forest fires.

Maia: Greek goddess of spring. Maia is the eldest of the Pleiades, and the mother of Hermes. A solitary goddess, she lives alone in a cave, and is associated with spring magick and midwifery. She aids vegetation and flowers in growth, and the land in fertility.

Malinalxochitl: Aztec Witch goddess. A great sorceress and ruler of magickal arts, Malinalxochitl controls snakes and scorpions. She has great power over life and death, and is skilled at crafting fantasies and hallucinations.

Mama Allpa, also *Allpamama:* Incan earth goddess. Mama Allpa is the patroness of fertility and the harvest. She is depicted with numerous breasts, indicating her powers of nourishment and motherhood.

Mama Cocha, **also** *Cochamama*: Incan goddess of the sea. The Incans honored Mama Cocha as the mother of the ocean and all the creatures within it. She protects fishermen and sailors, as well as providing prosperous blessings to anyone who makes their living from the sea.

Mama Oello, **also** *Ocllomama, Mama Ocllo:* Incan domestic goddess. Daughter of the sun and moon, Mama Oello taught the Incan people the arts of spinning and weaving. She is seen as the mother of warmth and self-preservation.

Mama Quilla, **also** *Mama Killa, Quillamama:* Incan goddess of time. Mama Quilla, "Mother Moon," rules the flow of time and is the creator and keeper of the Incan calendar. She protects married women from harm and deceit, and is connected with celebrations and festivals of all kinds. Mama Quilla is represented by a gold or silver disc imprinted with a woman's face.

Mami Wata: African goddess of water. Mami Wata is a water deity who visits her followers in dreams and hallucinations. She bestows wealth and healing on those who ask, and is known to curse the wicked with illness. Petitioners offer her perfume and sweet liquids. She appears as a mermaid, or as a beautiful woman dressed in red and white.

Mamlambo: African goddess of rivers. Mamlambo is the goddess of flowing waters in the Zulu tradition of Africa. She is depicted as a large, crocodile-type creature who drowns the unsuspecting and enjoys thunderstorms. If Mamlambo is caught, she is said to gift great wealth and abundance to her captors.

Manat: Arabian goddess of fate. Manat is the Crone aspect of the Triple Goddess, forming the triad with al-Uzza and al-Lat. She rules the flow of time, and controls the destiny of humanity. A powerful sorceress, Manat rules the mysteries of the Craft, divination, life, and death. Her symbols include the waning moon and black stones.

Manea: Italian goddess of the dead. Ruler of the underworld, Manea controls the night and the mysteries therein. She looks after spirits and ghosts, as well as those caught between life and death.

Mara: Latvian prosperity goddess. Mara rules all economic activities, specifically the bartering and trading of land or cattle. A household goddess, she is linked to domestic duties and child rearing.

Marama: New Zealand moon goddess. The Maori people honor the moon as Marama, a deity of light and resurrection. As a goddess of death, she collects the souls of humans, ensuring they do not return to the land of the living.

Marica: Italian goddess of rivers. Marica rules flowing waters and marshlands, as well as the animals who make their homes there. She is a powerful sorceress, prophetess, and enchantress, her spells and herbcraft capable of affecting both men and gods. Marica is the equivalent of the Greek Circe.

The Mar'rallang: Sister goddesses of Australia. The Mar'rallang are two identical sisters who have the same name and are married to the same man. They represent the duality within existence and the dichotomy of women, and act as a mirror to one another.

Marzanna, also *Morena:* Slavic goddess of winter. The ancient peoples of Poland created effigies of Marzanna out of straw and myrtle, ritually burning or drowning the doll to banish the cold of winter and welcome the warmth of spring. Marzanna rules the dark winter months as well as death, and is sometimes associated with Witchcraft and divination.

Mati-Syra-Zemlya: Slavic earth goddess. Mati-Syra-Zemlya translates as "Moist Mother Earth," and she is thought to be the most ancient of the eastern European deities. She is a wise prophetess, and allows petitioners to come to her without the aid of priestesses or shamans. Mati-Syra-Zemlya supplies abundant harvests, and is commonly offered hemp oil to invoke her blessings.

Matronae: The three goddess mothers of Europe. The Matronae are best known from the hundreds of altars found throughout Gaul (France), Spain, and Italy. They are depicted as three matronly figures surrounded by fruits, trees, children, and animals. The Matronae are the personification of motherhood, and are mainly seen as protective deities, guarding civilization from disease and starvation.

Matsu, also *Tian Hou, Mazu, Tien Hou:* Chinese goddess of the sea. Eastern Asians and Taoists honor Matsu as the ocean and guardian of fisherman and sailors. She is a deity of great kindness and compassion, spreading peace throughout the world. In some traditions she is also the Queen of Heaven who maintains the balance of masculine and feminine energies in the universe.

Mawu: West African moon goddess. Mawu rules the moon and the night sky, and is honored by the Fon people for the cool temperatures she brings. The essence of motherhood, she teaches her people to celebrate and revere the wisdom of their ancestors. Her twin and consort is the sun god Liza, and together they created the seven sets of twin deities who influence the world. Cowrie necklaces are sacred to Mawu.

Maya: Hindu goddess of illusion. Maya is the goddess of wisdom and intuition. She inspires the realization of the self, and is the embodiment of microcosm/macrocosm philosophy. Maya is the truth beyond the veil of existence, and she teaches that all energies are one. Associated with magick and Witchcraft, Maya is a creative power, manifesting nature from the power of her will.

Mayahuel: Aztec goddess of alcohol. Mayahuel is the many-breasted goddess of the agave bush, the plant from which tequila and pulque are derived. She is the mother of innumerable rabbit gods, and feeds her children pulque from her four hundred breasts, all of which produce the alcoholic beverage.

Mbaba Mwana Waresa: Rainbow goddess of Africa. The Zulu people of South Africa worship Mbaba Mwana Waresa for her creation of beer. She rules agriculture and harvests, as she has power over elemental water and earth. Also referred to as Lady Rainbow, Mbaba Mwana Waresa is the link between the gods and humanity, the bridge that crosses the realms. Her consort is a mortal named Thandiwe, who completed numerous legendary tasks at her request, in order to prove his worthiness of her.

Mboze: Central African goddess of agriculture. Mother of Bunzi, Mboze is the power of rainfall, harvests, and agriculture. She is seen as the mother of the Woyo people in the Democratic Republic of the Congo and Angola.

Medb, also *Maeve:* Intoxicating goddess of Ireland. Medb is a goddess of battle and is an expert warrior and huntress. She rules intoxicating substances, including alcohol and recreational drugs, particularly those that cause hallucinations. Known for her iron will and sexual promiscuity, Medb has many lovers and can sexually exhaust thirty men in one night. She is depicted with long, red hair, and is dressed in battle armor. Horses and bulls are her totems.

Medusa: Serpent goddess of Libya. Known throughout North Africa and Crete, Medusa is the keeper of feminine mysteries. She was imported to Greece as one the Gorgons, and morphed into a type of demon. Originally, she was the representation of life and death, a force that destroys in order to create. Medusa stands for balance within nature, and guards the thresholds of the earth, heaven, and the underworld. Her totem is the serpent, as it represents the endless cycle of death and rebirth. Medusa is depicted with snakes wrapped around her body and entwined in her hair, whispering secrets into her ears.

Meng-Po Niang Niang: Chinese goddess of reincarnation. Meng-Po Niang Niang resides in the underworld, distributing the Broth of

Oblivion to the dead. This liquid causes the souls to forget their previous lives, spiritually cleansing them for rebirth. She is the keeper of the past who purifies the mind and spirit so that previous sins will be forgiven.

Meskhenet, also *Mesenet, Meskhent:* Egyptian goddess of birth. Patroness of healers and midwives, Meskhenet rules the birthing process and children. She uses her powers of prophecy to divine an infant's destiny, and protects the child until adulthood. Her role as guardian continues in the afterlife, where Meskhenet assists with the soul's transition and rebirth into the underworld. She is represented by a woman's head on top of a birthing brick, upon which Egyptian women sat while giving birth.

Metis: Greek goddess of intelligence. A Titan goddess, Metis is the personification of feminine intuition. Her intelligence, craftiness, and wisdom outweigh that of all the gods. She is also seen as an oracle, and the patroness of counselors and therapists. Lover of Zeus; when a pregnant Metis predicted their children would be wiser than he, Zeus swallowed her whole. Athena was later born, bursting fully grown from Zeus's head. Metis remains in Zeus's belly, supplying him with inner wisdom and advice.

Mielikki, also *Annikki, Anna:* Finnish goddess of the hunt. Guardian of animals and a revered huntress, Mielikki rules forests and woodlands. She protects grazing animals and aids those who are lost in the wilderness. Her totem is the bear.

Minerva, also *Menrva:* Roman goddess of wisdom. Equated with Athena of Greece, Minerva is the goddess of knowledge and commerce. A virgin goddess, Minerva is only dependent upon herself, never taking a mate. She is a healing goddess and patroness of doctors and nurses. An inventor and alchemist, she is the creator of numbers, musical instruments, medicines, and machinery.

Minona: Protector goddess of West Africa. Minona is known as the caretaker of women by the Fon people. She blesses women with fertility and protects them from birth until death. She taught shamans divination through the use of palm kernels, and she can foresee the future.

Mokosh: Water and earth goddess of the Ukraine. Mokosh is worshipped in Slavic countries as the goddess of rain and fertile soil. She rules spinning, weaving, and domestic activities, as well as marriage rites and family affairs. She is associated with life-and-death matters, as she supplies the necessities of survival.

Momu: Scottish goddess of land. Momu rules wells, caves, and hillsides, and is thought to symbolize the power within the female form. She has authority over elemental earth and water, and is associated with fairies.

Morrigu, also *Morrigan:* Irish goddess of prophecy. With her sisters Badb and Macha, Morrigu forms a triad of war goddesses. She foretells the outcome of all battles, and is considered the Witch queen of death. She is the great sorceress of the Celts, her magickal powers of prediction and enchantment beyond compare. Morrigu also rules passionate love and sex, predominantly affairs that tend to have negative consequences. She is usually pictured as an attractive lady with long dark hair, or as an older woman in dark robes.

Mujaji: South African rain goddess. Mujaji rules rainfall and purification, as well as drought. She cleanses worshippers in preparation for ritual, and the people dance as an offering to her.

Mulhalmoni: Korean goddess of magickal healing. Patroness of women healers and shamans, Mulhalmoni is a water goddess who controls the power of spiritual and physical sight. She is invoked to heal eye ailments and blindness. She holds the veil over the third eye, removing the boundary from her priestesses when asked.

Musso Koroni: Chaos goddess of West Africa. The first woman created by the gods, Musso Koroni is the Daughter of the Void, doomed to forever wander the earth. She creates sadness, disorder, and anger among humanity. Her totem is the leopard.

Mut: Egyptian mother goddess. Mut is the divine mother and queen of the gods, and the embodiment of universal mysteries. Mother of Nut, she is a sky deity and represents the power within all living things. She fiercely protects Egypt and its inhabitants, granting ultimate authority unto the reigning pharaoh. Mut is depicted as a woman with white vulture wings on her crown or on her back.

Nammu: Sumerian creator goddess. Nammu is the mother of heaven, earth, and the sea, spontaneously creating the universe without the aid of a mate. She is the life-giving water that sustains humanity as well as the gods, and is attended by seven other goddesses who act as handmaidens.

Nana Buluku: West African goddess of making. The Fon people worship Nana Buluku as the primordial creator goddess and grandmother of the gods. She is also seen as the first woman of the Yoruba religion, life breathed into clay by the Great Gods. She rules herbs, spellcraft, and magick, and is pictured carrying a basket full of bark and roots. Mandrake root is sacred to her.

Nanshe: Dream goddess of Babylonia. Nanshe is a water goddess of prophecy worshipped throughout Mesopotamia. She is referred to as the Interpreter of Dreams, and she blesses her priests with soothsaying abilities. Nanshe's symbols include jars of water and fish.

Nantosuelta: Celtic goddess of nature. Nantosuelta rules fertility, agriculture, and the home. She supplies prosperity and contentment within domestic affairs, and is often depicted holding a model house in her hands.

Nehallenia: Celtic goddess of abundance. Nehallenia is known throughout various regions as a deity of abundance and fertility. She protects those who travel by sea, and devotees light candles to her in gratitude for their safe journeys. She supplies civilization with food and banishes poverty. Nehallenia is depicted as a young woman holding foodstuffs on her lap.

Neith, also *Nit:* Domestic goddess of Egypt. Mother of Ra, Neith was born from the ancient waters of creation. She is the guardian of women, and protects the bonds of marriage. She rules the war, hunting, and the art of weaving, including the bandages and shrouds of the dead. Neith is pictured as a woman holding a bow and arrow or a weaving shuttle.

Nekhebet: Egyptian goddess of protection. Nekhebet is the protector of Upper Egypt, guardian of women in labor, and nursemaid to children of royal birth. She is one of the two Ladies of Pharaoh along with Wadjet, and is the force behind the reigning pharaoh's strength and power. She is depicted as a woman with the head of a vulture.

Nemesis: Greek goddess of vengeance. Nemesis is the goddess of indignation and revenge. Her name means "She Who Deals Out," and she punishes those who experience undeserved happiness or excessive good luck. Nemesis hunts the wicked in order to distribute justice, and she is the force of karma within Greek society. Her symbols are the sword and the scales.

Nephthys: Egyptian goddess of the dead. Nephthys is the shadow of her sister Isis, and rules the darkness and the secrets of death. She is the Lady of the Temple, the protector of souls and queen of the underworld. She has great magickal power, and though it is generally rooted in darkness, she offers the gloriousness of rebirth to the deceased.

Nerthus: Germanic goddess of the earth. Honored in northern Europe, Nerthus blesses civilization with prosperity and happiness. She is also considered one the Vanir deities, and is associated with earth magick and fertility.

Ngame: West African goddess of the soul. The Akan people in Ghana see Ngame as a moon deity, and believe she created the celestial planets. She gave humans souls by shooting lunar rays into them at birth with a bow and arrow. Girls who were thought to be blessed with Ngame's mystical powers were raised as royalty, and became the ruling queens and priestesses of their people.

Nike: Greek goddess of victory. Nike is the personification of success, specifically in battle and sports competitions. She is usually depicted at the side of Athena, holding a palm branch.

Ningal: Sumerian goddess of languages. Ningal is the goddess of interpretation and insight. She reveals the meaning of dreams and oracular phrases, as well as deciphering forgotten languages and misunderstood texts. Also a love deity, Ningal evolves from the maiden bride of the moon god to the mother of Inanna, and embraces the role by teaching her daughter all she knows about marriage, sexuality, and the feminine mysteries.

Ninhursag: Great goddess of Sumeria. Worshipped in all of Mesopotamian society and sects, Ninhursag is the primordial mother who created humanity from clay. She is identified with serpents and cows, and she nourishes the universe with the milk from her breast. A healing goddess, she rules herbal medicine and all forms of vegetative fertility. Her name translates as "Lady of the Mountain."

Ninkasi: Sumerian goddess of alcohol. Ninkasi is the mother of beer, created by Ninhursag to heal and to satisfy the desires of the heart. She rules unheeded passion and self-assurance, and is offered perfumes and fresh water by her devotees.

Ninlil: Sumerian goddess of birth. Ninsun was repeatedly raped (some say seduced) and impregnated by her husband, Enlil, who disguised himself as water spirits and guardians. She had three children from these interludes, and thereby became the mother of the moon, the rivers, and the underworld. Ninlil is a goddess of barley and vegetation, and she aids in healing barrenness and infertility. She helps women heal from the terror of rape and leads them to wholeness.

Ninsun: Mesopotamian goddess of knowledge. Ninsun is primarily a Sumerian deity, though some scholars believe her to be a reflection of the Babylonian Gula. Her name means "Lady Wild Cow," and she was worshipped by farmers and herdsmen to bless their animals and crops. In the *Epic of Gilgamesh*, Ninsun is depicted as the hero's mother and counselor. She is the keeper of wisdom, and an interpreter of dreams.

Ninti: Sumerian goddess of life. Ninti is a goddess of healing and childbirth. Her name translates as "Lady of the Rib" or "Lady of Life." She creates the bones of infants from their mother's ribs, which were considered the bones of life in ancient Sumer. Ninti heals broken bones and illnesses related to the skeletal frame.

Nirriti: Hindu goddess of misery. Nirriti is the epitome of death, disease, and misfortune. Dark magick and Witchcraft are derived from her, as well as poverty and all types of mishaps and bad luck. She is the shadow and opposing force of Lakshmi, and the embodiment of all sin.

The Norns: Norse goddesses of fate. Urd, Verthandi, and Skuld form the triad that is the Norns. They sit beneath the World Tree and spin the threads of destiny and fate for mortals and the gods. They water and prune the tree, helping it stay healthy and green. As the goddesses of time, the Norns represent the past, present, and future.

Nu Kua: Chinese goddess of creation. It is Nu Kua who creates order from the primordial chaos of the universe, setting the land, sea, and sky into place. She molded the first humans from clay, and established the laws of marriage and society. She is depicted as half woman, half dragon or as a mermaid.

Nuneh: Armenian goddess of hearth and home. Nuneh is the guardian of the household and the family; she protects children and the elderly. She is a wise goddess who blesses petitioners with practical knowledge and common sense.

Nut: Egyptian goddess of the stars. Nut is the lady of the sky and nightfall. She rules the celestial bodies and is the barrier that separates order from primeval chaos. She uses her powers of resurrection and rebirth to give birth to the sun each day. Mother of Isis, Nut is depicted as a woman clothed in stars, standing on tiptoe and arching her body to cradle the earth. Her hands and feet are believed to be the four cardinal directions.

Oba: Yoruban goddess of rivers. Oba is a West African goddess, worshipped primarily in Nigeria and also in the Santerían and Yoruban New World traditions. She forms a triad with Oshun and Oya. Oba is the power of flowing water, representing the inevitable flow of time and life, and the movement of energy. She is the dutiful wife who shows honor and loyalty to her husband, even when it is undeserved.

Odudua, **also** *Odua:* Yoruban goddess of love. Odudua is worshipped in West Africa as the mother of love and child rearing. Her name means "Black One," and she is pictured as a great beauty with skin like obsidian stone. She rules directional and elemental south, and devotion in romantic relationships. Women celebrate Odudua's feast days by offering themselves with abandon to male worshippers.

Oenothea: Greek goddess of wine. A hearth and home deity, Oenothea rules the making and drinking of wine. She is the hostess or the innkeeper who opens the home to the weary and needy, sharing her abundance with all.

Onatha: Iroquois goddess of the harvest. Some Native Americans celebrate Onatha as the maiden goddess of wheat and the harvest. She was abducted by evil spirits and carried to the underworld. The sun produced a heat wave to rescue her, drying out the soil, which allowed Onatha to rise from the earth and bloom into freedom.

Ops: Roman goddess of agriculture. Ops rules fertility and vegetation, supplying the earth with abundant harvests and wealth. She is a nurturing goddess, teaching humanity to properly care for crops and how to reap and sow accordingly.

Oshun: Yoruban goddess of pleasure. Oshun's worship spread from West Africa to the New World, where she is honored in Santerían traditions. She rules all bodies of water and all sensual acts. Patroness of women and Witches, Oshun is hedonistic in nature, taking part in any activity that embraces joy and pleasure. Jewelry, perfumes, dancing, and seashells are sacred to her. Oshun is generally depicted as a dark-skinned woman with large hips. She forms a triad with Oba and Oya.

Oya: Yoruban goddess of weather. Oya is the personification of wind and storms, ranging from gentle breezes to hurricanes, depending on her temper. She vehemently protects women from conflict and poverty. She is the power of change and transformation, and is often depicted carrying a sword or machete to cut away the past and make way for the future. Oya is also a goddess of commerce, supplying marketplaces and retail business with wealth and success.

Pachamama, also *Mamapacha:* Incan earth goddess. Pachamama is an earth and agricultural deity who sends earthquakes when humanity fails to honor her. She is pictured as a dragon that sleeps beneath the mountains of Peru and supplies the earth with the nourishment it needs to survive. She is offered cornmeal daily to ensure an abundance of food and water among her people. Llamas and guinea pigs are sacred to her.

Pajau Yan: Moon goddess of Vietnam. Pajau Yan is the goddess of health and healing. She aides the deceased in their transition to the underworld by granting them the mystical flowers of peace.

She supplies good fortune to the living, and is said to live in the moon.

Pani: New Zealand goddess of vegetation. The Maori people honor Pani as their goddess of plants and fertility. She gave birth to the yam, which is one of the most important crops of the Polynesian islands.

Papatuanuku: Maori Earth Mother. The Maori of New Zealand worship Papatuanuku as the mother of humanity, animals, and woodlands. She supplies the earth with food, and parents offer their children's allegiance to her in gratitude. When Papatuanuku is forcibly separated from the embrace of her consort Rangi Nui, her anger causes earthquakes.

Parvati, **also** *Uma:* Hindu goddess of femininity. Parvati represents the beauty of womanhood, and is the Maiden aspect of the Triple Goddess, forming the triad with Durga and Kali Ma. Skilled and patient, Parvati seduces the god Shiva with her beauty, charm, and wit, manipulating him into telling her the secrets of the cosmos. She is the patroness of artists, dancers, and poets. Her name means "She Who Is of the Mountains," and Parvati is usually pictured as a beautiful young woman dressed in green.

Pasiphae: Moon goddess of Crete. A three-faced deity, Pasiphae was originally the great goddess of Crete and a powerful Witch and oracle. She rules the sun and is worshipped during equinoxes and solstices. Over time, Pasiphae was transformed into the immortal wife of King Minos and sorceress mother of the monstrous Minotaur.

Pax: Roman goddess of peace. Pax is the personification of peace. She bestows contentment and joy, and is invoked during barters and negotiations. Pax is pictured holding olive branches or a staff.

Pele: Volcano goddess of Hawaii. Pele can take many forms, but she is most recognizable in her guise of a beautiful young woman. In this form, she is capable of seducing any male: mortal or god.

She rules elemental fire and all the aspects thereof, including transmutation, and is known for her volatile temper.

Pereplut: Slavic goddess of fortune. Pereplut rules the powers of fate and destiny. She distributes both good and bad fortune to humanity, and is invoked through libations, preferably drunk from a hollowed horn.

Persephone: Greek goddess of spring. Daughter of Demeter, Persephone is the spring maiden, a deity of growth and happiness. She rules agriculture and represents the innocence and purity of youth. In her role as the Dark Maiden, Persephone is the queen of the underworld and the keeper of souls. She embodies the wisdom of life and death, and is skilled in magick and divination in all its forms.

Pinga: Inuit goddess of protection. Inuits honor Pinga as the guardian of souls, for she escorts the deceased to the underworld. She created medicine to heal the sick, and she supplies food as the goddess of the hunt and wild game.

Po Ino Nogar: Rice goddess of Cambodia. Po Ino Nogar controls rainfall and protects fields from drought and disease. She gifted humanity with rice and fertile soil, in addition to the skills to cultivate the land. Her symbols are water and clouds.

Pomona: Roman goddess of agriculture. Pomona cares for fruit trees, orchards, and gardens. She teaches the proper care of blossoming plants and promotes agricultural fertility. Apples and the pruning fork are her symbols.

Proserpina: Roman goddess of spring. The equivalent of the Greek Persephone, Proserpina is the goddess of seasonal spring and maidenhood. She rules growth and agriculture, and is the representation of the blooming earth. As the Dark Maiden, she is the wife of Pluto and rules the underworld by his side as the keeper of ghosts.

Psyche: Greek goddess of the soul. Psyche is the guardian of the human soul, ensuring humanity's need for love and happiness is met. She rules the growth of loving relationships from infatuation to true love, and promotes an enduring spirit. Psyche is the representation of every woman's transformation from the innocent woman into the mature woman. She is depicted as a beautiful woman with the wings of a butterfly or bird.

Pukkeenegak: Inuit domestic goddess. The Inuit people worship Pukkeenegak as a hearth and home goddess. She rules all domestic tasks including sewing and cooking. As a deity of childbirth, she rules all stages of pregnancy, including conception and labor.

Purandhi: Indian goddess of familial blessings. In Hindu mythology, Purandhi is the goddess of marriage, family, and children. She controls childbirth and the abundance within the family and household, including inheritances.

Radha: Hindu goddess of love. Radha is the personification of love between humanity and God, as well as between woman and man. She is the loyal devotee and celestial wife of the god Krishna. Radha teaches the joys of affection, faith, unwavering devotion to the self, and divinity.

Rán: Norse goddess of the sea. Rán is a water deity, ruling the oceans and storms. She reigns over the underworld found at the bottom of the sea, and she collects the souls of the drowned in her fishing nets. Her daughters are the waves of the ocean, and Rán works with them to sink ships to the depths of the sea.

Rangda: Demon goddess of Bali. Rangda is evil incarnate and the queen of Witches and ghosts. She possesses righteous people and drives them to sinful behavior. Although she is constantly defeated by the forces of good, Rangda always returns to battle again. She is associated with the sea, and is depicted as a naked old woman with dirty hair, sharp teeth, and a tongue that reaches her knees.

Rati: Sex goddess of Bali. The Hindus of Bali worship Rati as the goddess of sex and lust. She controls passion in romantic relationships and is invoked to help one attain an unrequited love.

Red Tara: Tibetan goddess of transformation. The goddess Tara is worshipped in many forms throughout Eurasia, and in the Hindu and Buddhist traditions. The Red Tara rules over physical, mental, and spiritual transformation. She magnifies all positive intentions and actions, and transmutes wild emotions into effective reasoning. She is the power of desire and passion, and she controls magick and alchemical processes.

Renenet: Egyptian goddess of the name. Renenet is known as the Lady of the Double Granary, a title that pays respect to her roles as protector of the harvest and prosperity matriarch. Also referred to as She Who Rears, Renenet watches over infants and children, gifting newborns with a secret name that grants strength and guards them from harm.

Rhea: Greek goddess of time. Titan mother of the Olympian gods, Rhea represents the flow of time and the power of ancestral blessings. Her name means "ease," and her calming essence relieves the suffering and chaos in the world. Menstrual blood and milk are sacred to her, demonstrating her power as a feminine fertility figure.

Rhiannon: Welsh goddess of patience. Rhiannon is the great queen of Wales and a lunar deity. She relieves suffering and pain, her singing lulling the living into a peaceful sleep and comforting the souls of the dead. She is the creator of magickal enchantments and dream work. Rhiannon's mythology tells of her patiently enduring seven years of punishment after she is falsely accused of murdering her son. She is one of the five goddesses of Avalon, along with Blodeuwedd, Arianrhod, Branwen, and Cerridwen.

Saga: Scandinavian goddess of history. Saga resides in the Sökkvabekkr, a large hall located under a river, whose walls flow with mead. A goddess of tales and myths, she drinks heavily from her walls and transcribes the important events of the day so that none will be forgotten. She is the patroness of seers and writers, and she records the history of the world as well as events to come. She is known throughout Norse and Germanic societies; scrolls and mead are sacred to her.

Samovila: Slavic goddess of woodlands. Samovila rules the forest and protects the animals that live within woodlands. She causes great harm to anyone who abuses her creatures. A shapeshifter, she can transform herself into any animal, and she teaches the skill to the devoted and faithful. Her knowledge of plants and herb medicine makes Samovila a favorite among kitchen Witches.

Sangiyan Sari: Rice goddess of Indonesia. The people of the Celebes Islands in Indonesia worship Sangiyan Sari as an earth goddess. She gifted humanity with fertile soil and rice crops, keeping starvation and famine at bay.

Saranyu: Hindu goddess of animals. Saranyu is the mother of all animals, including mythic creatures. She is the consort of the sun god Surya, and is worshipped as the clouds and the dawn. When she grew tired of the heavens and her husband, she turned herself into a horse and ran away. Saranyu is often depicted with the attributes of a mare.

Sarasvati: Hindu goddess of words. Sarasvati is the creator of the arts, including music, dancing, and poetry. She is the maker of sciences and mathematics, invented the Sanskrit language, and rules all aspects of teaching and learning. Referred to as "The Flowing One," Sarasvati inspires devotees to great heights in intellectual and creative endeavors. She is depicted as a white-skinned woman, usually with a peacock.

Satine: Underworld goddess of Indonesia. As a goddess of the afterlife, Satine is said to reside on the Ninth Mountain in the underworld.

Souls must climb the other eight before they are permitted to look upon her.

Saule: Baltic sun goddess. Saule is the mother of the planets and the embodiment of the sun. She ensures the growth of vegetation as well as household prosperity. She is associated with the sea and with the underworld; the light she emits is a representation of hope during difficult times. Saule is pictured with long golden hair, and serpents are sacred to her.

Scathach: Celtic warrior goddess. Scathach is a warrior and teacher of the art of war. She instructs young men in martial arts and swordplay, as well as initiating them into sexual experience. She has the gift of foresight and the power to grant wishes. Her name translates as "Shadowy One" or "She Who Strikes Fear."

Sedna: Inuit goddess of the underworld. Sedna rules the ocean depths and the sea creatures within. She was sacrificed by her father and sank to the bottom of the sea—her severed body parts transforming into seals, whales, and walruses. As these animals are staples of survival in Inuit society, Sedna is also seen as the mother of the hunt and a deity of endurance. She lives in the underworld at the bottom of the ocean, and has power over life and death.

Sekhmet: Punishing goddess of Egypt. Sekhmet is referred to as the Eye of Ra, as she is the personification of the God's anger. Her role as both a creative and destructive force aligns her with women, as she represents the fire of femininity. Sekhmet protects women, bestows inner balance, and stands for righteous anger. She is depicted as a full-figured woman with the head of a lion.

Selene: Greek goddess of the moon. Selene is the Titan goddess of the moon, and rules lunar magick. She aids in sleep and in dream prophecy, as well as with sensual acts. She is usually depicted riding a horse or chariot, with a crescent-moon crown.

Sengdroma: Tibetan goddess of animals. Sengdroma protects herds of animals from harm, and is honored by farmers and hunters. She is pictured as having the face of a lion.

Seshat: Egyptian goddess of writing. Creator of hieroglyphics, Seshat rules the written word in all its forms. She invented measurements and calculations, and as such is the patroness of architects and accountants. Seshat is the guardian of books and the goddess of history. Scrolls, pens, and scales are sacred to her.

Sgeg Mo Ma: Tibetan goddess of beauty. Sgeg Mo Ma rules the physical and spiritual aspects of feminine beauty. She is often depicted holding a magickal mirror, in which she can see the tangible force of beauty as well as the inner well of the soul.

Shakti: Ultimate goddess of India. Shakti is the primal force of female energy found within each goddess. She is the ancient force of power, the breath and the will that animates the divine Devi. Shakti liberates women from the trivial events of everyday life, and leads them to enlightenment. Her creative abilities and transcendent power are the core of every Hindu goddess. She is the force in yoga practices and in tantric rituals.

Shamhat: Erotic goddess of Mesopotamia. Known throughout all of Mesopotamian civilization, Shamhat is the High Priestess of Inanna who rules over the sacred marriage rites and erotic acts. She holds the power of the divine mysteries, and brings about the physical and mental transformation of puberty. Shamhat teaches the art of sensuality, as well as the rules and manners required in high society.

Shasti: Hindu goddess of children. Shasti protects mothers in labor and children until they reach puberty. She is a favorite of midwives and nurses, and is pictured as a matronly figure riding a cat.

Sheela Na Gig: Irish hag goddess. Sheela Na Gig is best known from the stone carvings found throughout Ireland that depict a nude female figure exposing her vulva. She is the lustful hag, the Dark Crone goddess, and the epitome of the feminine mysteries of life and death. Sheela Na Gig holds in her hands the laughter and passion of existence, and the pain and fear of death, upholding the cycle of birth, death, and rebirth.

Shekinah: Queen goddess of the Middle East. Originally Shekina was an extension of Asherah and Astarte's worship in Canaan. She evolved over time to become the consort and force of the Hebrew god as described in the Kabbalah. Shekinah is now honored as the Queen of Heaven and the feminine aspect of the God. She is the Divine Mother who heals the heart and protects humanity from evil.

Shitala, also *Sheetala:* Hindu goddess of disease. Shitala is a pestilence deity and a healing force in the Hindu pantheon. She created smallpox and a variety of other diseases, and only she has the power to cure the ailing. She despises filth and dirt, and those who wish her blessings must be ritually cleansed—their bodies as well as their homes.

Siduri Sabitu: Babylonian goddess of immortality. Siduri Sabitu guards the entrance to the Garden of the Gods, ensuring no mortals enter the forbidden paradise. She distributes the wine of immortality to the Divine, and is associated with sacred waters and the sea.

Sif: Norse goddess of grain. Patroness of farmers, Sif rules the harvest and the cultivation of land. She is a prophetess, enchantress, and a shapeshifter. Wife of the god Thor, Sif is pictured with long golden hair representing fields of wheat.

Sigyn, also *Sigunn:* Norse goddess of endurance. Wife of the trickster god Loki, Sigyn is known for her compassionate nature and gentle temperament. She represents patience and familial loyalty, especially in times of turmoil.

Sita: Hindu goddess of virtue. Sita is a daughter of the earth and the personification of womanly ideals in Hindu society. When kidnapped and held prisoner, Sita not only refused the advances of her wealthy captors, but she maintained her chastity of spirit as well. She controls elemental fire—an ability gained by her successful completion of the *Agni Pariksha,* or trial by fire. Sita rules wisdom, and she embodies divine patience.

Sjöfn: Norse goddess of love. Sjöfn uses magickal herbs, potions, and musical enchantment to coerce women and men to fall in love. She removes fear and past regrets from the heart and inspires passion for the opposite sex. Sjöfn also ensures love lasts between married couples, and calms the emotions during arguments and disputes.

Skadi: Winter goddess of Scandinavia. Skadi rules the winter season and the darkness that comes with it. She bestows justice and vengeance as necessary on the wicked, and is the incarnation of righteous anger. As the mistress of the hunt, Skadi gave humanity the bow and arrow. Snow-covered mountains are her home, and Scandinavia is thought to be named for her.

Snake Woman, **also** *Minoan Snake Woman:* Goddess of Crete. While many historians believe Snake Woman to be a household and fertility deity, other sources cite her as High Goddess and Priestess of Crete, and a powerful, seductive sorceress. She represents the feminine mysteries and holds all the magickal powers of the serpent. Her statuette depicts her in Minoan dress with her breasts exposed, and snakes in each hand.

Sól: Norse goddess of the sun. Sól rides across the sky in a chariot every morning from east to west. The golden glow of her beauty and power warms and nourishes the earth.

Sophia: Goddess mother of the Middle East. In Gnostic and Judeo-Christian traditions, Sophia is the Divine Feminine and the Holy Spirit of the Christian trinity. She is the voice and the wisdom of God, and a piece of her is said to reside in every human. As God's true source of power, Sophia is the mother of all creation and the universe. Her totem is the dove.

Spider Woman: Creatrix goddess of Native America. Spider Woman is known by many Native American peoples as the Great Teacher, the Creator of Life, and the weaver of dreams. She is the guardian of all existence on earth, and she uses her power to weave the fabric of time and to bind physical reality to the unknown.

Sulis: Healing goddess of Britain. Worship of Sulis was widespread throughout British, Roman, and Celtic lands. Though she is a solar deity, Sulis rules elemental water and aids in healing diseases and ailments. She rules purification and the healing of the mind, body, and spirit.

Sura, also *Varuni:* Hindu goddess of wine. Sura rules intoxication and fermented fruits. She blends the immortality to be distributed among the gods and worthy mortals. She guides devotees to transcendent wisdom through the imbibing of sacred wines or nectars.

Tabiti: Scythian goddess of the hearth. Tabiti is a fire goddess worshipped in eastern Eurasia. She is a protector of animals and the wealth of herders and farmers. As a goddess of the home, Tabiti ensures familial loyalty and promises prosperity to a well-functioning household.

Tap Tun: Phallic goddess of Thailand. Tap Tun's temple in Bangkok is filled with lingams as tools for phallic worship. She is the energy force within males, specifically within the penis, and controls lust, passion, and impotence.

Tashmetum: Babylonian love goddess. Tashmetum rules love within the bonds of marriage, and can lead women to their true mate. Her name means "She Who Grants Requests," and her followers invoke her to answer prayers of all natures. She is the mediator between mortals and the gods, as well as between husbands and wives. Tashmetum is the height of womanly virtue, the seductress and the loyal wife. She and her husband, Nabu, are often invoked together for matters of love.

Tawaret: Protection goddess of Egypt. Tawaret protects the world from the evil influence of her consort Apep. She is the aggressive guardian of pregnant women and of those in labor, driving evil spirits away from the mother and child. Her name translates as "She Who Is Great," and she is depicted as half crocodile, half pregnant hippopotamus.

Tefnut, also *Tefenet:* Egyptian goddess of water. Also known as "She of Moisture," Tefnut rules all aspects of water, including humidity and drought. She has associations with both the sun and moon, and is occasionally pictured as a lioness as an expression of her volatile temper. She was created by the god Alum from his mucus, and her name is thought to mean "spat waters."

Teteoinnan: Aztec goddess of midwives. Teteoinnan is the mother of the gods and the patroness of midwives, physicians, and holistic intuitives. She invented medicine and rules herbal curatives, making her a vegetation deity as well. Teteoinnan is celebrated during harvest festivals with blood sacrifices in fields. She is the Mother aspect in a triad with Tlazolteotl and Tozi.

Thalassa: Greek goddess of the sea. Thalassa is the primordial essence of the ocean. She is the mother of fish and sea mammals, and her body and womb are considered to be the sea itself.

Thalia: Blooming Greek goddess. One of the Three Graces, Thalia is the goddess of springtime and thriving vegetation. She rules festivals and banquets, and represents the fruitful abundance of the earth.

Themis: Greek goddess of divine justice. Themis is the Titan goddess of order and law, and a seer of future events. She is the force of tradition and customs, and rules hospitality and morality. Themis is the patroness of oracles and intuitives, specifically those who seek to use their gifts to uphold and teach divine laws. She is depicted as a blindfolded woman, holding a balanced set of scales.

Tiamat: Chaos goddess of Babylon. Tiamat is the ancient mother of the gods in Babylonian tradition. She is the force of chaos that was split in two to form the heavens and the earth. She rules salt waters and is described as a great dragon.

Tlalteuctli: Aztec earth goddess. Tlalteuctli is the Dark Mother of the earth, the fertile soil that feeds life and embraces death. The world was created from pieces of her dismembered body after she was attacked by fellow deities. The Aztec people buried human hearts in the earth and watered soil with blood to honor Tlalteuctli.

Tlazolteotl: Aztec goddess of filth. Tlazolteotl controls pestilence, sin, and disease, including STDs. She also rules sexual misconduct, such as adultery and rape. She is the Dark Maiden who inspires sin, but also cleanses it away. Those who confessed their misdeeds were purified by Tlazolteotl's priests as a type of rebirthing ritual; those who lied were sentenced to death. She forms a triad with Tozi and Teteoinnan.

Tozi, **also** *Toci:* Aztec goddess of healing. Tozi is the patroness of women healers and the guardian of the sweat lodge and bath rituals. She rules purification of the physical and spiritual bodies, and heals illness and disease. Tozi is the grandmother spirit and caretaker of nature. She is the Crone aspect of the Triple Goddess, forming the triad with Tlazolteotl and Teteoinnan.

Tsovinar: Armenian goddess of water and fire. Created from fire, Tsovinar rules heat and warmth, and holds control over bodies of water and rain. A temperamental deity, it is she who frightens the waters of heaven and sends them to earth, creating the Great Flood.

Tuonetar: Finnish goddess of the dead. Tuonetar is the queen of the underworld and keeper of the dead. She separates lovers by sending death to one of the pair, then captures the soul and traps it within the underworld.

Tyche: Greek goddess of fortune. Tyche is the goddess of chance and prosperity. Her reign extends from success in business dealings to luck with gambling. She guides the financial affairs of the world and is often depicted with Nemesis, who balances the distribution of Tyche's blessings.

Uni: Supreme goddess of Italy. The Etruscans saw Uni as the ultimate feminine deity. She rules every aspect of a woman's life, paying special attention to marriage rites and pregnancy. She protects women from harm, heartbreak, and infidelity. Hera and Juno are considered her equivalents.

Ushas: Hindu goddess of the dawn. Ushas rides a chariot across the sky every morning, bringing light to the world. She awakens the divine potential in humanity and in the gods, offering spiritual enlightenment to those who seek it. Her name is Sanskrit for "dawn," and she wards off evil. She is sometimes symbolized as a flock of birds.

Uttu: Sumerian goddess of domestic arts. Seen as the model for the perfect wife, Uttu rules the household and the art of weaving. She aids in difficult childbirths and is skilled in herb medicine. Uttu represents the "behind-the-scenes" power that resides behind every successful marriage and prosperous husband.

Uzume: Japanese goddess of laughter. Uzume is the full-figured goddess of happiness and femininity. She is the embodiment of energy in action, and gives birth to light and hope. When Amaterasu hides herself away in a cave, it is Uzume who entices her out by performing a lewd, comical dance. Bells and dancing are sacred to her.

Vac: Hindu goddess of speech. Ruler of sound and the spoken word, Vac is the patroness of writers, teachers, and artists. She is the source of creation, the sacred word that was the beginning of all existence and all knowledge upon the earth. Vac is the personification of thoughts manifesting into reality.

The Valkyries: Norse goddesses of the dead. Lead by Freya, the Valkyries are a group of beautiful shapeshifting goddesses. They are Odin's messengers and act as psychopomps, escorting slain warriors to the afterlife. They are of an unknown number, and are considered fierce warriors with control over the elements.

Vammatar: Finnish goddess of disease. Daughter of Tuonetar, Vammatar rules all aspects of pain and suffering from disease. Although she dispenses discomfort, she can aid the afflicted through illness, strengthening the body and immune system so that healing may commence. She is often depicted with her sister Kipu-Tytto.

Var: Covenant goddess of Scandinavia. Var rules all oaths and contracts, paying special attention to agreements between men and women. She is traditionally invoked on wedding days, and she punishes those who break their promises. Her power is derived from the energy of spoken words, as they bind the speaker to truth and honor.

Vasudhara: Abundance goddess of Nepal. Vasudhara is the goddess of good fortune and wealth, and rules all types of abundance and prosperity. Women petition her to bless their wombs and their fields with fertility. She is pictured as having six arms holding sacred objects and mudras, and is thought to be the equivalent of the Hindu Lakshmi.

Ved'Ma: Slavic goddess of storms. Ved'Ma is a Witch goddess in eastern Europe who transforms from young and beautiful to old and hag-like. She controls the waters of life and death, and is the bringer of storms and floods. Ved'Ma is also an enchantress, reigning over magickal herbs and plants.

Vellamo: Finnish goddess of the sea. Pictured as a mermaid, Vellamo rules the oceans and rivers. She is a great seductress, manipulating men and gods into illicit affairs. She is the power of the sea, and the mistress of fish.

Venus: Roman goddess of love. The equivalent of the Greek Aphrodite, Venus is the goddess of love, sex, and beauty. She is the morning and the evening star, and the daughter of the sea. Venus dispels troubles and turmoil, gifting devotees with happiness and joy. She is the patroness of prostitutes, and heals sexual issues on the mental and physical levels.

Vesna: Russian goddess of spring. Vesna is an oracular goddess, said to live at the top of a mountain. She is the personification of spring and controls the survival of plants and crops. She is celebrated at the end of February with song and dance to welcome springtime.

Vesta: Roman goddess of hearth and home. Vesta is the virgin goddess of the household and of fire. She is an earth deity as well, controlling the domestic arts, including cooking and cleaning. Her presence within the home is said to bind a family together, and the ancient Romans made a daily offering to her. Vesta is the equivalent of the Greek Hestia.

Vila: Slavic nature goddess. Vila is a nature deity of eastern Europe. She is the protector of animals and woodlands, and has the knowledge of magickal herbs. Vila can shapeshift into any animal she chooses, and can teach this skill to devotees. If any mortal harms one of her sacred animals, Vila will lure the offender into a sacred circle and dance them to death.

Wadjet: Egyptian goddess of protection. Wadjet is a goddess of childbirth, specifically guarding children of royalty and means. She protects Lower Egypt and instills her wisdom and skill into the ruling pharaoh. She is one of the two Ladies of Pharaoh along with Nekhebet. Wadjet is celebrated on December 25th with chants and songs. The cobra is her totem.

Wakahirume: Japanese goddess of weaving. Wakahirume is the favorite weaving maiden of Amaterasu. She creates dreams and visions, and has connections to fate and time. She died after puncturing her vagina on her weaving shuttle, symbolizing the death of innocence and maidenhood after sexual intercourse.

White Buffalo Calf Woman: Mother goddess of Native America. White Buffalo Calf Woman is known by many Native Americans. She taught the people agriculture and the basics of survival, as well as the sacred rituals and ceremonies to enrich their lives. As the nourishing goddess, she appears as the buffalo, offering her flesh and hide to the tribe so that they may live and flourish.

White Tara: Tibetan goddess of mercy. The goddess Tara is worshipped in many forms throughout Eurasia, and in the Hindu and Buddhist traditions. In her manifestation of White Tara, she guides humanity to the wonders of the afterlife and teaches the mysteries of existence. She leads civilization to understanding and tolerance, as well as healing the spirit or body as needed. The White Tara is the embodiment of compassion, and she is said to answer all prayers.

Xi Hou: Chinese goddess of light. Xi Hou is the mother of the ten suns that light the earth in rotation. She represents the renewal of a new day, carefully caring for and nurturing the light and power so that it offers all opportunities to humanity. Xi Hou is associated with prosperity and luck, and her symbol is gold.

Xochiquetzal: Aztec goddess of love. Goddess of women, Xochiquetzal rules love and marriage. She is the patroness of sacred prostitutes, artists, and dancers. As a lunar deity, she controls transformation, weaving, and magick. Xochiquetzal is depicted as a beautiful young woman in gold and expensive clothes. Marigolds and doves are sacred to her.

Yama No Kami: Japanese goddess of the hunt. Yama No Kami is the guardian of women and the mother of seasonal time. She rules the forests and mountains, and hunters honor her for gifting them with prey.

Yaoji: Chinese goddess of the mountains. Yaoji is a sorceress specializing in love potions. She is worshipped as the rocks and mountain peaks. She wields power over dreaming, and sends messages to her followers in visions. Revered for her wisdom, Yaoji teaches the magickal properties of herbs and magickal brewing.

Yaya Zakurai: Japanese goddess of spring. Yaya Zakurai brings seasonal spring to the earth each year. She is celibate until the flowers begin to bloom; she then takes many lovers among mortals and gods. Yaya Zakurai is represented by the cherry tree and blossoms.

Yellow Tara: Tibetan goddess of prosperity. The goddess Tara is worshipped in many forms throughout Eurasia, and in the Hindu and Buddhist traditions. The Yellow Tara rules wealth and abundance in both the spiritual and the physical worlds. She provides prosperity of all types to humanity, intent on destroying poverty and ignorance.

Yemaya, also *Yemoja, Iemanja:* African goddess of water. Yemaya is honored throughout West Africa and the Caribbean as the mother of the sea and the moon. She is the keeper of the female mysteries and a guardian of women. She aids in the conception of children and their births, protecting and blessing infants until they hit puberty. She is a healing goddess, showing compassion and kindness to those in need. Yemaya is the personification of rivers and bodies of water, and is often depicted as a mermaid.

Yondung Halmoni: Air goddess of Korea. Yondung Halmoni is the ruler of wind and storms. She is honored during shamanic rituals as a deity of change and transformation. Petitioners offer her rice cakes to receive her blessings.

Yuki Onne: Japanese goddess of death. Yuki Onne is the Snow Maiden, a deity of winter and blizzards. She is the brokenhearted and scorned woman, betrayed by her husband and left with a cold, empty heart. She brings freezing death to those suffering from the chill of winter as well as those made cold by bitterness, lulling them to an eternal sleep with a song. She gifts an easy and painless death, and guides the soul to the underworld.

Yum Chenmo, also *Prajnaparamita:* Tibetan goddess of wisdom. Yum Chenmo is considered the female Buddha, and the mother of transcendental knowledge. She balances the laws of the universe and offers enlightenment to the diligent. She is the abyss, the All and the Nothing, and is the embodiment of teaching and meditation.

Zaramama, also *Mamazara:* Incan goddess of agriculture. Zaramama is a goddess of grain and the mother of corn. She supplies the earth and its people with nourishment and food. She is depicted as a woman with ears of corn as a part of her features, wrapped in a silver-clasped shawl.

Zaria, also *Zoria, Zorya:* Slavic goddess of beauty. Zaria rules the morning and the dawn. She is the heavenly bride, the symbol of the perfect mortal wife, as she is pure, honorable, and of great beauty. Zaria is depicted as the morning star.

The Zorya: Slavic goddesses of time. The Zorya are a triad of goddesses who control time and protect the world from evil and Armageddon. They represent the dawn, noon, and the evening as well as past, present, and future. Their names are Zorya Utren-nyaya, Zorya Vechernyaya, and Zorya Polunochnaya.

Zywie: Polish goddess of healing. Zywie is the bringer of death and the giver of life in Slavic mythology. She blesses the ill with regeneration and health, and gifts spiritual rebirth to those in need. Her totem is the cuckoo bird.

TWO

. . . . ✳ . . . .

Attributes

Abundance

Abundantia

Aje

Al-Lat

Amashilamma

Anna Perenna

Anuket

Aphrodite

Artemis

Asase Yaa

Atira

Bast

Bona Dea

Chicomecoatl

Copia

Corn Woman

Coventina

Dana

Demeter

Don

Dugnai

Epona

Erce

Ertha

Feronia

Flidais

Fortuna

Freya

Frigga

Gaia

Habondia

Hathor

Hecate

Ishtar

Isis

Kali Ma

Lajja Gauri

Lakshmi

Lama

Lilith

Mati-Syra-Zemlya

Matronae

Mawu

Mayahuel

Nehallenia

Nerthus

Ninsun

Ops

Pachamama

Pax

Pele

Pomona

Proserpina

Purandhi

Radha

Shakti

Shekinah

Sita

Thalia

Tlalteuctli

Tozi

Tyche

Vasudhara

Venus

White Buffalo Calf Woman

Yellow Tara

Yemaya

Zaramama

ADDICTIONS

Baba Yaga

Demeter

Ereshkigal

Kali Ma

Lilith

Morrigu

Sekhmet

Shakti

Shekinah

The Valkyries

AGING

Asase Yaa

Baba Yaga

Bugady Musun

Cerridwen

Elli

Ereshkigal

Estsanatlehi

Gaia

Hel

Hestia

Ix Chel

Kali Ma

Maia

Mawu

Maya

Nana Buluku

Ninhursag

Pele

Shakti

Skadi

Snake Woman

Ved'Ma

Yaya Zakurai

AGRICULTURE

Aine

Ala

Anuket

Asase Yaa

Asherah

Ashnan

Atira

Axomama

Bachué

Beiwe

The Bereginy

Brigid

Bunzi

Ceres

Chalchiuhtlicue

Corn Woman

Demeter

Dziewanna

Eostre

Epona

Erce

Euphrosyne

Flora

Freya

Gaia

Habondia

Hecate

Inari

Inkosazana

Isis

Ix Chel

Jord

Lady of Beasts

Madre Vieja

Mara

Mbaba Mwana Waresa

Minona

Onatha

Ops

Pachamama

Pax

Persephone

Po Ino Nogar

Pomona

Proserpina

Rhea

Sangiyan Sari

Shakti

Shitala

Sita

Vesna

White Buffalo Calf Woman

Xochiquetzal

Yama No Kami

Zaramama

ANGER, AGGRESSION

Black Tara

Blue Tara

The Erinyes

Hera

Indrani

Kali Ma

Oya

Pele

Shakti

Tiamat

Tsovinar

Uni

Wadjet

ANIMALS

Aine

Anahit

Ardwinna

Artemis

Artio

Athene

Atira

Bast

Beiwe

The Bereginy

Brigantia

Britomartis

Bugady Musun

Caipora

Cerridwen

Coatlicue

Cybele

Diana

Dziewanna

Epona

Flidais

Freya

Gula

Hecate

Inanna

Ishtar

Kunapipi

Lady of Beasts

Lupa

Malinalxochitl

Mara

Marica

Medusa

Mielikki

Mut

Papatuanuku

Pasiphae

Rhiannon

Samovila

Saranyu

Sedna

Sekhmet

Sengdroma

Shakti

Snake Woman

Spider Woman

Tabiti

Tlalteuctli

Vila

Wadjet

White Buffalo Calf Woman

Yama No Kami

ARBITRATION

Asherah

Athene

Demeter

Iris

Kuan Yin

Lama

Meskhenet

Nemesis

Nike

Oshun

Shakti

Shekinah

Tashmetum

ARCHITECTURE

Athene

Isis

Minerva

Seshat

Shakti

ARTS AND CRAFTS

Amaterasu Omikami

Astghik

Athene

Bast

Benten

Brigid

Brogla
Calliope
Cerridwen
Eostre
Erzulie
Hathor
Hecate
Hina
Hine
Inanna
Isis
Ix Chel
Minerva
Morrigu
Oshun
Sarasvati
Shakti
Sheela Na Gig
The Valkyries
Vesna
Xochiquetzal

ASTRAL TRAVEL

Baba Yaga
Cerridwen
Ereshkigal
Isis
Kali Ma
Nephthys

Nut
Pele
Shakti

ASTROLOGY

Al-Uzza
Astarte
Astraea
Atargatis
Cerridwen
Hathor
Inanna
Ix Chel
Kali Ma
Lajja Gauri
Minerva
Mut
Nut
Seshat
Shakti

ATHLETICS

Artemis
Athene
Elli
Ereshkigal
Feronia
Nike
Shakti

AUTHORITY

Anath

Artemis

Asherah

Athene

Banba

Druantia

Ereshkigal

Ériu

Fódla

Hathor

Hebat

Hel

Hera

Hine

Hsi Wang Mu

Isis

Juno

Lady of Beasts

Lakshmi

Lilith

The Mar'rallang

Matsu

Medb

Minerva

Morrigu

Mujaji

Mut

Ninhursag

Ninlil

Ninsun

Oya

Pele

Sekhmet

Shakti

Shekinah

Snake Woman

Sophia

Uni

BALANCE

Agemem

Ch'ang O

Demeter

Durga

Fravashi

Gyhldeptis

Hine

Ishtar

Kali Ma

Lada

Ma'at

Mami Wata

The Mar'rallang

Mawu

Mokosh

Mut

Onatha

Persephone

Proserpina

Shakti

Shekinah

Spider Woman

Tlalteuctli

BANISHING

Akewa

Marzanna

Red Tara

Sigyn

BEAUTY

Aglaia

Amaterasu Omikami

Anahit

Aphrodite

Astarte

Astghik

Bast

Bixia Yuanjin

Branwen

Chalchiuhtlicue

Dziewanna

Eostre

Erzulie

Estsanatlehi

Euphrosyne

Freya

Hathor

Hebat

Hina

Inanna

Indunn

Isis

Ix Chel

Lada

Lakshmi

Lilith

Maia

Mami Wata

Onatha

Oshun

Parvati

Persephone

Proserpina

Psyche

Radha

Sarasvati

Sgeg Mo Ma

Shakti

Sif

Snake Woman

Ushas

Venus

Vesna

Xochiquetzal

Yaya Zakurai

Yemaya

Zaria

Beginnings, new

Ananke

Anapel

Ausrine

Bixia Yuanjin

Branwen

Brigid

Chalchiuhtlicue

Coventina

Dana

Danu

Eostre

Hathor

Isis

Kali Ma

Kuan Yin

Lada

Mbaba Mwana Waresa

Nammu

The Norns

Oshun

Oya

Pele

Pomona

Shakti

Shekinah

Tiamat

Vesna

Birth Control

Astarte

Carmenta

Juno

Mami Wata

Nephthys

Vesna

Blessings

Aphrodite

Asase Yaa

Aziri

Brigid

Corn Woman

Erce

Estsanatlehi

Fravashi

Green Tara

Hestia

Inanna

Isis

Kuan Yin

Lada

Lama

Mami Wata

Minona

Oshun

Pele

Shakti

Sheela Na Gig

Shekinah

White Tara

Yemaya

BLOOD

Anath

Blodeuwedd

Chicomecoatl

Coatlicue

Durga

The Erinyes

Estsanatlehi

Kali Ma

Medusa

Morrigu

Pele

Sekhmet

Shakti

Shitala

Skadi

Tlalteuctli

The Valkyries

BOUNDARIES

Akewa

Ananke

Durga

Hera

Juno

Kamrusepas

Lady of Beasts

Nephthys

Nut

Shakti

Shekinah

Tawaret

Uni

BREWING, ALCOHOL, BEER/MEAD

Asherah

Ashnan

Demeter

Gunnlod

Hathor

Kamui Fuchi

Mamlambo

Mati-Syra-Zemlya

Mayahuel

Mbaba Mwana Waresa

Nephthys

Ninkasi

Pereplut

Saga

Sekhmet

Shakti

Snake Woman

The Valkyries

BREWING, MAGICKAL

Arianrhod

Baba Yaga

Cailleach

Cerridwen

Ereshkigal

Erzulie

Gullveig

Hecate

Holda

Isis

Meng-Po Niang Niang

Momu

Morrigu

Nephthys

Rangda

Sjöfn

Tiamat

Yaoji

BUSINESS SUCCESS

Abundantia

Aje

Armathr

Artemis

Aziri

Eostre

Hera

Isis

Juno

Lakshmi

Mara

Minerva

Nehallenia

Oya

Shakti

Sheela Na Gig

Uni

Yellow Tara

CALM, REST

Asase Yaa

Blue Tara

Ereshkigal

Inanna

Kali Ma

Kamrusepas

Mawu

Nu Kua

Onatha

Pax

Persephone

Proserpina

Sekhmet

Shakti

White Tara

CEMETERIES

Cerridwen

Coatlicue

Ereshkigal

Hecate

Hel

Inari

Kali Ma

Lilith

Morrigu

Nephthys

Oya

Persephone

Proserpina

Shakti

The Valkyries

CHANGE

See TRANSFORMATION

CHAOS

Cerridwen

Coyolxauhqui

Danu

Ereshkigal

The Erinyes

Eurynome

Gaia

Ix Chel

Kali Ma

Marzanna

Musso Koroni

Oya

Pele

Sekhmet

Shakti

Tiamat

The Valkyries

Yemaya

CHASTITY

Al-Uzza

Artemis

Astraea

Athene

Bona Dea

Britomartis

Chasca

Diana

Dziewanna

Eostre

Hestia

Kupala

Lajja Gauri

Minerva

Sedna

Shakti

Shekinah

Sita

Venus

Yaya Zakurai

Zaria

CHILDBIRTH, MIDWIVES / BIRTH

Akhushtal

The Akkan

Alemona

Anahit

Anapel

Artemis

Asherah

Candelifera

Carmenta

Chalchiuhtlicue

Chihucoatl

Coatlicue

Coventina

Diana

Ereshkigal

Erua

Freya

Frigga

Hathor

Haumea

Hecate

Hekit

Hera

Hine

Isis

Ix Chel

Juno

Lada

Lady of Beasts

Leto

Lilith

Lucina

Meskhenet

Nekhebet

Nephthys

Ninti

Oshun

Pukkeenegak

Purandhi

Renenet

Shakti

Shasti

Snake Woman

Tabiti

Tawaret

Teteoinnan

Tlazolteotl

Tozi

Uni

Wadjet

Xochiquetzal

Yemaya

CHILDREN

Akhushtal

The Akkan

Akwaba

Ala

Alemona

Artemis

Asase Yaa

Asherah

Bast

Bixia Yuanjin

Carmenta

Chasca

Chihucoatl

Demeter

Eostre

Erua

Haumea

Hecate

Hekit

Isis

Itzpapalotl

Juno

Kikimora

Kuan Yin

Kupala

Lady of Beasts

Leshachikha

Lilith

Lucina

Lupa

Mara

Matronae

Meskhenet

Nekhebet

Ninti

Papatuanuku

Pukkeenegak

Renenet

Rhea

Shakti

Shasti

Shitala

Tabiti

Tawaret

Vesna

Wadjet

Yemaya

CIVILIZATION

Ala

Alemona

Anuket

Asase Yaa

Atargatis

Athene

Auchimalgen

Banba

Bast

Brag-srin-mo

Chihucoatl

Demeter

Eka Abassi

Ériu

Fódla

Gula

Hathor

Hestia

Hine

Ilmatar

Inanna

Isis

Kali Ma

Lady of Beasts

Mboze

Nammu

Nana Buluku

Ninhursag

Nu Kua

Odudua

Oshun

Papatuanuku

Po Ino Nogar

Sarasvati

Shakti

Snake Woman

Tlalteuctli

The Valkyries

White Buffalo Calf Woman

CLARITY

Baba Yaga

Candelifera

Cerridwen

Ereshkigal

Hecate

Inanna

Medb

Nu Kua

Sgeg Mo Ma

Shakti

Shekinah

COMMERCE

Aje

Armathr

Aziri

Hera

Inari

Isis

Juno

Mara

Minerva

Nehallenia

Oya

Shakti

Uni

Yemaya

COMMUNICATION

Atargatis

Hecate

Hina

Iris

Isis

Koevasi

Kuan Yin

Lady of Beasts

Ma'at

Mawu

Minerva

Ninhursag

Pax

Sarasvati

Shakti

Spider Woman

Tefnut

Vac

The Valkyries

COMPASSION

Aine

Amaterasu Omikami

Anuket

Astraea

Bixia Yuanjin

Devi

Eostre

Gbadu

Hestia

Iris

Isis

Kuan Yin

Leto

Ma Gu

Matsu

Ninlil

Pachamama

Pajau Yan

Rati

Rhiannon

Saule
Shakti
Shekinah
Sophia
White Tara
Yemaya

CONFIDENCE

Bia
Cailleach
Hine
Juno
Matsu
Parvati
Psyche
Red Tara
Shakti
Shekinah

CONTRACTS

Artemis
Athene
Baba Yaga
Hecate
Isis
Minerva
Nu Kua
Saga

Shakti
Var

COSMOS

Agemem
Al-Uzza
Anahit
Ananke
Arianrhod
Astraea
Ausrine
Blodeuwedd
Chomo-Lung-Ma
Coatlicue
Danu
Devi
Ereshkigal
Eurynome
Frigga
Gaia
Gleti
Gula
Inanna
Ishtar
Kali Ma
Manat
Maya
Mut
Nammu

Nut

Pasiphae

Shakti

Shekinah

Sophia

Spider Woman

Tiamat

White Tara

The Zorya

COURAGE

Artemis

Artio

Baba Yaga

Bia

Black Tara

Branwen

Durga

Hine

Inanna

Isis

Kali Ma

Matsu

Morrigu

Nanshe

Parvati

Red Tara

Shakti

Sita

Uzume

The Valkyries

Yama No Kami

CREATION / CREATIVITY

Agemem

Ala

Al-Lat

Ananke

Andraste

Aphrodite

Arachne

Ararat

Asase Yaa

Astarte

Bachué

Bast

Biliku

Brag-srin-mo

Brigid

Canola

Ceres

Cerridwen

Chihucoatl

Coatlicue

Danu

Druantia

Durga

Eostre

Etugen

Eurynome

Gaia

Hathor

Hecate

Hina

Hine

Hsi Wang Mu

Ilmatar

Inanna

Isis

Ix Chel

Izanami

Kali Ma

Koevasi

Lady of Beasts

Lajja Gauri

Mawu

Maya

Mboze

Medusa

Mut

Nammu

Nana Buluku

Neith

Ninhursag

Nu Kua

Papatuanuku

Radha

Sarasvati

Shakti

Shekinah

Sophia

Spider Woman

Thalassa

Tiamat

Vesna

Yemaya

Yum Chenmo

CROSSROADS

Baba Yaga

Cerridwen

Chihucoatl

Demeter

Hecate

Kali Ma

Morrigu

Oba

Onatha

Persephone

Proserpina

CUNNING, CHARM

Anath

Aphrodite

Arianrhod

Athene

Baba Yaga

Ereshkigal

Gaia

Gunnlod

Gyhldeptis

Hera

Inari

Isis

Kali Ma

Metis

Oya

Shakti

Sheela Na Gig

Snake Woman

Tap Tun

Uni

Uzume

The Valkyries

Venus

DANCE

Anahit

Bast

Benten

Brogla

Calliope

Cybele

Devi

Eostre

Ereshkigal

Erzulie

Estsanatlehi

Eurynome

Hathor

Hi'iaka

Isis

Kali Ma

Lada

Lakshmi

Mami Wata

Oshun

Pele

Samovila

Sarasvati

Shakti

Snake Woman

Uzume

Vesna

Vila

Xochiquetzal

Yemaya

DARKNESS

Baba Yaga

Cailleach

Cerridwen

Ereshkigal

Estsanatlehi

Hecate

Hel

Hine

Isis

Izanami

Kali Ma

Koliada

Lilith

Marzanna

Morrigu

Nephthys

Nirriti

Onatha

Persephone

Proserpina

Satine

Shakti

Sheela Na Gig

Skadi

DAWN

Ararat

Aurora

Ausrine

Beiwe

Bixia Yuanjin

Chasca

Eostre

Estsanatlehi

Evaki

Gaia

Saranyu

Shakti

Shekinah

Tawaret

Ushas

Uzume

Wakahirume

Zaria

The Zorya

DEATH

The Akkan

Ala

Arianrhod

Artemis

Asase Yaa

Auchimalgen

Baba Yaga

Badb

Cailleach

Cerridwen

Chicomecoatl

Chihucoatl

Coatlicue

Coyolxauhqui

Cybele

Ereshkigal

Estsanatlehi

Faumea

Freya

Frigga

Hecate

Hel

Hine

Ishtar

Ixtab

Izanami

Kali Ma

Kikimora

Kipu-Tytto

Lamia

Lilith

Manea

Mara

Marama

Marzanna

Medb

Medusa

Morrigu

Nanshe

Nantosuelta

Nekhebet

Nephthys

Nirriti

The Norns

Onatha

Pele

Persephone

Proserpina

Rán

Rangda

Satine

Sedna

Shakti

Sheela Na Gig

Sophia

Tuonetar

The Valkyries

Vammatar

Ved'Ma

Yuki Onne

The Zorya

Zywie

DECEIT

Apate

Baba Yaga

Blodeuwedd

Ereshkigal

Hera

Medb

Morrigu

Nirriti

Oya

Uni

The Valkyries

DECISIONS

Artemis

Baba Yaga

Ereshkigal

Fravashi

Hecate

Isis

Kali Ma

Lilith

Ma'at

Morrigu

Neith

Ninhursag

The Norns

Shakti

Sulis

DESTINY

The Akkan

Ananke

Anapel

Badb

Bixia Yuanjin

Carmenta

Enekpe

Ereshkigal

Freya

Frigga

Inanna

Isis

Kali Ma

Kuan Yin

Mama Quilla

Manat

Mawu

Meskhenet

Ninlil

The Norns

Pereplut

Shakti

Shekinah

DESTRUCTION

Artemis

Astarte

Badb

Bellona

Cailleach

Cerridwen

Chalchiuhtlicue

Coatlicue

Coyolxauhqui

Ereshkigal

The Erinyes

Hecate

Kali Ma

Lilith

Macha

Marzanna

Medusa

Morrigu

Musso Koroni

Ningal

Nirriti

Oya

Pele

Persephone

Proserpina

Rán

Rangda

Sekhmet

Shakti

Skadi

Tlalteuctli

Ved'Ma

DIPLOMACY

Anath

Athene

Demeter

Ereshkigal

Hebat

Hecate

Hera

Hsi Wang Mu

Isis

Lady of Beasts

Medb

Minerva

Morrigu

Neith

Oshun

Sekhmet

Shakti

Shekinah

The Valkyries

Uni

DISASTER

Baba Yaga

Badb

Bellona

Circe

Coatlicue

The Erinyes

Hecate

Kali Ma

Lilith

Macha

Morrigu

Musso Koroni

Nirriti

Oya

Rán

Shakti

The Valkyries

Vammatar
Ved'Ma

DISCIPLINE

Artemis
Athene
Baba Yaga
Cerridwen
Dewi Nawang Sasih
Hecate
Hera
Kikimora
Ma'at
Medb
Nu Kua
Shakti
Uni
Yama No Kami

DISEASE, ILLNESS

Artemis
Bast
Black Tara
Cailleach
Cerridwen
Ereshkigal
The Erinyes
Kuan Yin
Lilith

Nirriti
Hecate
Hel
Kali Ma
Kipu-Tytto
Sekhmet
Tlazolteotl
Vammatar

DIVINATION

Acpaxapo
Akonadi
Andraste
Anna Perenna
Atargatis
Baba Yaga
Branwen
Brigid
Cerridwen
Corra
Devi
Eostre
Erzulie
Gullveig
Hathor
Hecate
Ishtar
Isis
Ix Chel

Kali Ma

Lilith

Mami Wata

Mati-Syra-Zemlya

Medb

Minona

Morrigu

Ngame

Ningal

Ninsun

The Norns

Oshun

Shakti

Sheela Na Gig

Shekinah

Snake Woman

Spider Woman

Teteoinnan

Yemaya

DIVINE COMMUNICATION

Acpaxapo

Brigid

Ertha

Fravashi

Iris

Kamui Fuchi

Kuan Yin

Lama

Nephthys

Shakti

Shamhat

Shekinah

Sophia

Spider Woman

The Valkyries

DIVINE INTERVENTION

Blue Tara

Devi

Durga

Ereshkigal

Ertha

Fravashi

Lama

Meskhenet

Nephthys

Shakti

Shekinah

Snake Woman

Sophia

DREAMS

Cerridwen

Chuang Mu

Epona
Ereshkigal
Hathor
Hecate
Isis
Kikimora
Lilith
Mami Wata
Maya
Morrigu
Nanshe
Ngame
Ningal
Ninsun
Onatha
Persephone
Proserpina
Rhiannon
Shakti
Sheela Na Gig
Shekinah
Snake Woman
Spider Woman
The Valkyries
Yaoji

EARTHQUAKES

Asase Yaa
Bona Dea

Ereshkigal
Kali Ma
Mahuika
Oya
Pachamama
Papatuanuku
Pele
Persephone
Proserpina
Shakti

ECLIPSE

Cerridwen
Gleti
Ix Chel
Kali Ma
Lilith
Mama Quilla
Mawu
Pajau Yan

ELOQUENCE

Aglaia
Aphrodite
Bixia Yuanjin
Calliope
Devi
Eostre
Ereshkigal

Erzulie

Hathor

Hina

Isis

Kuan Yin

Ma Gu

Oshun

Pajau Yan

Rhiannon

Shakti

Shekinah

Venus

Zaria

Enchantments

Aphrodite

Arianrhod

Baba Yaga

Brigid

Cerridwen

Circe

Eir

Eostre

Ereshkigal

Freya

Frigga

Gula

Gullveig

Hathor

Hecate

Hera

Holda

Isis

Marica

Minona

Morrigu

Odudua

Onatha

Persephone

Proserpina

Rangda

Red Tara

Shakti

Sheela Na Gig

Sif

Sjöfn

Snake Woman

Spider Woman

Tap Tun

Uni

Vesna

Endings

Anath

Baba Yaga

Cerridwen

Ereshkigal

Izanami

Kali Ma

Morrigu

The Norns

Onatha

Oya

Pele

Persephone

Proserpina

Shakti

Tiamat

The Valkyries

Yaya Zakurai

ENLIGHTENMENT

Baba Yaga

Bast

Black Tara

Blue Tara

Cerridwen

Fravashi

Green Tara

Kuan Yin

Mawu

Red Tara

Shakti

Shekinah

Sophia

White Tara

Yellow Tara

EXORCISM

Auchimalgen

Black Tara

Cerridwen

Ereshkigal

Hecate

Hel

Holda

Iris

Ixtab

Mami Wata

Manea

Morrigu

Nephthys

Nut

Oya

Pinga

Rán

Satine

Saule

Shakti

Sheela Na Gig

Skadi

Themis

Tuonetar

The Valkyries

The Zorya

Zywie

FAITH

Aglaia

Amaterasu Omikami

Chun T'i

Devi

Diana

Fravashi

Inanna

Isis

Kali Ma

Kuan Yin

Lakshmi

Shekina

Sophia

White Buffalo Calf Woman

White Tara

FAMILY

Asase Yaa

Brag-srin-mo

Branwen

Ceres

Chantico

Corn Woman

Demeter

Enekpe

Fravashi

Haltia

Hathor

Hestia

Holda

Isis

Kamui Fuchi

Kuan Yin

Lamia

Lofn

Mami Wata

Matronae

Matsu

Nana Buluku

Nekhebet

Nuneh

Onatha

Pachamama

Persephone

Po Ino Nogar

Proserpina

Rhea

Shakti

Sif

Sita

Vesta

The Zorya

FATE

Anahit

Ananke

Arachne

Astraea

Atargatis

Cerridwen

Fravashi

Gbadu

Gula

Hecate

Heimarmene

Inanna

Juno

Kali Ma

Mama Quilla

Manat

Maya

Meskhenet

Mokosh

Morrigu

Ninlil

The Norns

Pereplut

Renenet

Shakti

Spider Woman

Tyche

The Valkyries

FEAR

Baba Yaga

Banka-Mundi

Cerridwen

Ereshkigal

Green Tara

Hecate

Ishtar

Izanami

Kali Ma

Medb

Morrigu

Nirriti

Onatha

Persephone

Proserpina

Sedna

Shakti

Snake Woman

The Valkyries

FERTILITY

Aine

Ala

Al-Lat

Anahit

Aphrodite

Arianrhod

Artemis

Asase Yaa

Astarte

Atargatis

Athene

Atira

Banka-Mundi

Bast

Beiwe

Blodeuwedd

Boann

Bona Dea

Brag-srin-mo

Cerridwen

Coatlicue

Danu

Demeter

Devi

Druantia

Dzydzilelya

Eostre

Erce

Faumea

Feronia

Flora

Freya

Frigga

Gaia

Hathor

Haumea

Hecate

Hina

Inanna

Isis

Ix Chel

Lada

Lady of Beasts

Lajja Gauri

Lakshmi

Madre Vieja

Mama Allpa

Mama Oello

Mati-Syra-Zemlya

Matronae

Mawu

Mayahuel

Mbaba Mwana Waresa

Mokosh

Morrigu

Nammu

Nana Buluku

Nanshe

Nerthus

Ninhursag

Onatha

Ops

Pachamama

Parvati

Persephone

Po Ino Nogar

Rangda

Renenet

Saule

Shakti

Shasti

Sheela Na Gig

Shitala

Sif

Snake Woman

Tawaret

Tefnut

Tlazolteotl

Vesna

Yemaya

FESTIVALS / PARTIES

Aphrodite

Bast

Bona Dea

Cybele

Eostre

Erzulie

Hathor

Isis

Nephthys

Nut

Oshun

Rhea

Shakti

Thalia

Uzume

Vesna

FIDELITY

Athene

Chup Kamui

Dzydzilelya

Hera

Juno

Mami Wata

Ningal

Papatuanuku

Parvati

Pasiphae

Shekinah

Sigyn

Sita

FLOWERS

Aine

Aphrodite

Blodeuwedd

Chicomecoatl

Creddylad

Dziewanna

Eostre

Flora

Freya

Hathor

Kupala

Lada

Lakshmi

Maia

Malinalxochitl

Onatha

Pele

Persephone

Proserpina

Shakti

Venus

Vesna

Xochiquetzal

Yaya Zakurai

FOOD

Aha Njoku

Amashilamma

Annapatni

Axomama

Bugady Musun

Dewi Nawang Sasih

Dugnai

Erce

Inari

Inkosazana

Mara

Mielikki

Papatuanuku

Po Ino Nogar

Sangiyan Sari

Zaramama

FORESIGHT

Acpaxapo

Akonadi

Antevorta

Baba Yaga

Badb

Cerridwen

Ereshkigal

Freya

Gullveig

Indrani

Isis

Lamia

Mati-Syra-Zemlya

Medusa

Meskhenet

Minona

Morrigu

Nanshe

The Norns

Saga

Shakti

Shekinah

Snake Woman

Vesta

FORGIVENESS

Blodeuwedd

Demeter

Gula

Hecate

Hestia

Hina

Ishtar

Isis

Kuan Yin

Ninlil

Pachamama

Pax

Rhiannon

Shekinah

Sigyn

Sophia

Tlazolteotl

FORTUNE, LUCK

Abundantia

Aspelenie

Benten

Bixia Yuanjin

Blue Tara

Ch'ang O

Erzulie

Isis

Lajja Gauri

Lakshmi

Lama

Mami Wata

Manat

Nemesis

Ops

Pajau Yan

Pereplut

Pomona

Renenet

Saule

Shakti

Tyche

Venus

Yama No Kami

FREEDOM

Aphrodite

Artemis

Athene

Baba Yaga

Baubo

Bixia Yuanjin

Black Tara

Bona Dea

Branwen

Ch'ang O

Diana

Dziewanna

Feronia

Hecate

Heimarmene

Isis

Ix Chel

Kali Ma

Lajja Gauri

Ma Gu

Medb

Minerva

Saranyu

Shakti

Sheela Na Gig

Uttu

Vesta

FRIENDSHIPS

Aphrodite

Baubo

Eostre

Gula

Hathor

Hecate

Hi'iaka

Inari

Ishtar

Juno

Lady of Beasts

Lofn

Sif

Uzume

GAMBLING

See FORTUNE, LUCK

GATES, CAVES, PORTALS, AND DOORWAYS

Amaterasu Omikami

Carna

Cerridwen

Cybele

Demeter

Dike

Ereshkigal

Faumea

Fravashi

Hecate

Hina

Inanna

Inari

Kamui Fuchi

Lama

Momu

Nephthys

Nut

Onatha

Pele

Persephone

Proserpina

Shakti

Sheela Na Gig

Siduri Sabitu

Sulis

The Valkyries

The Zorya

Grief, Sadness

Aine

Angerona

Anna Perenna

Blodeuwedd

Branwen

Ceres

Cerridwen

Coatlicue

Demeter

Ereshkigal

Erzulie

Hecate

Inanna

Isis

Kali Ma

Kuan Yin

Lamia

Morrigu

Musso Koroni

Nirriti

Onatha

Oshun

Persephone

Proserpina

Sedna

Shakti

Tiamat

Yemaya

Guardians

Al-Uzza

Bast

Bugady Musun

Enekpe

Ereshkigal

Fravashi

Gunnlod

Hathor

Hi'iaka

Idunn

Inari

Ishtar

Kuan Yin

Lama

Matsu

Nephthys

Shakti

Sheela Na Gig

Siduri Sabitu

Snake Woman
Spider Woman
Sulis
Tawaret
Wadjet
The Zorya

GUIDANCE

Candelifera
Cerridwen
Gaia
Holda
Isis
Juno
Kali Ma
Kuan Yin
Lama
Ngame
Ninlil
Pinga
Shakti
Shekinah
Siduri Sabitu
Sophia
Spider Woman

GUILT

Blodeuwedd
The Erinyes
Erzulie
Ma'at
Rhiannon
Tlazolteotl

HANGOVERS

Asherah
Ashnan
Demeter
Euphrosyne
Gunnlod
Hathor
Kamui Fuchi
Mamlambo
Mati-Syra-Zemlya
Mayahuel
Mbaba Mwana Waresa
Nephthys
Ninkasi
Pereplut
Sekhmet
Shakti
Snake Woman
The Valkyries

Happiness, Joy

Aphrodite

Bast

Baubo

Cocomama

Eostre

Ertha

Erzulie

Euphrosyne

Eurynome

Green Tara

Hathor

Hina

Isis

Kuan Yin

Lada

Ma Gu

Mawu

Ningal

Ninkasi

Oshun

Radha

Rhea

Saule

Shakti

Shekinah

Skadi

Snake Woman

Thalia

Uzume

Vesta

Harvest

Amaterasu Omikami

Anath

Asase Yaa

Ashnan

Atira

Bachué

The Bereginy

Bunzi

Ceres

Demeter

Dziewanna

Erce

Feronia

Gaia

Habondia

Leshachikha

Mama Allpa

Mati-Syra-Zemlya

Mawu

Mbaba Mwana Waresa

Ninhursag

Ops

Onatha

Persephone

Po Ino Nogar

Proserpina
Renenet
Shakti
Sif
Tawaret

Healing

Airmed
Aja
Arnamentia
Artemis
Asase Yaa
Black Tara
Bona Dea
Brigid
Carna
Cerridwen
Coventina
Dana
Devi
Eir
Gula
Haltia
Hecate
Hi'iaka
Idunn
Isis
Ix Chel
Kamrusepas

Kuan Yin
Ma Gu
Mami Wata
Minerva
Mokosh
Mulhalmoni
Nana Buluku
Neith
Ninkasi
Ninti
Pachamama
Pajau Yan
Pinga
Samovila
Sekhmet
Shakti
Shekinah
Shitala
Snake Woman
Sulis
Teteoinnan
Tlazolteotl
Tozi
Uzume
Vammatar
Venus
White Buffalo Calf Woman
White Tara
Yaoji

Yemaya

Zywie

Health, mental

Baba Yaga

Beiwe

Black Tara

Cocomama

Eir

The Erinyes

Hecate

Idunn

Isis

Kamrusepas

Kuan Yin

Mami Wata

Medb

Oya

Pajau Yan

Saule

Sekhmet

Shakti

Shekinah

Sulis

Uzume

Venus

White Buffalo Calf Woman

Zywie

Health, physical

Artemis

Black Tara

Carna

Cerridwen

Cocomama

Eir

Gula

Idunn

Inari

Kamrusepas

Kuan Yin

Ma Gu

Mami Wata

Mokosh

Mulhalmoni

Nephthys

Ninti

Pajau Yan

Pinga

Saule

Sekhmet

Shakti

Shitala

Sulis

Uzume

Vammatar

Venus

Zywie

HEARTH & HOME

Akwaba

Aspelenie

Athene

Baba Yaga

Bast

Brigid

Ceres

Chantico

Demeter

Dugnai

Epona

Feronia

Frigga

Haltia

Hecate

Hestia

Isis

Juno

Kamui Fuchi

Kikimora

Mara

Mokosh

Nantosuelta

Neith

Nu Kua

Nuneh

Oenothea

Pukkeenegak

Saule

Shakti

Shitala

Sif

Snake Woman

Tabiti

Tawaret

Tlazolteotl

Uttu

Venus

Vesta

Xochiquetzal

Yemaya

HEAVEN

Al-Lat

Amaterasu Omikami

Anath

Asherah

Don

Gula

Hathor

Hebat

Hecate

Hera

Inanna

Ishtar

Isis

Izanami

Juno

Kuan Yin

Lajja Gauri

Matsu

Nephthys

Nut

Shakti

Shekinah

Sophia

Uni

Ushas

The Valkyries

Wadjet

Kupala

Lada

Ma Gu

Marica

Mayahuel

Mielikki

Nana Buluku

Pasiphae

Pinga

Samovila

Shakti

Vila

Yaoji

Herbs

Airmed

Aja

Ashnan

Baba Yaga

The Bereginy

Ceres

Cerridwen

Circe

Demeter

Eir

Haumea

Hecate

Idunn

Kamrusepas

Hindsight

Acpaxapo

Akonadi

Badb

Cerridwen

Gullveig

Indrani

Isis

Morrigu

The Norns

Saga

Shakti

Sophia

Yemaya

HOMOSEXUALITY

Bast

Cybele

Erzulie

Lakshmi

Shakti

Tap Tun

HUNTING

Andraste

Artemis

Athene

Atira

Banka-Mundi

Bendis

Britomartis

Dziewanna

The Erinyes

Flidais

Frigga

Hecate

Neith

Pinga

Sedna

Shakti

Skadi

The Valkyries

Yama No Kami

ILLUSIONS

Artemis

Baba Yaga

Cerridwen

Circe

Diana

Eostre

Ereshkigal

Flidais

Haumea

Hecate

Inari

Isis

Kali Ma

Marica

Maya

Morrigu

Oshun

Oya

Parvati

Samovila

Shakti

The Valkyries

Vila

IMPOTENCE

Anuket

Aphrodite

Eostre

Ereshkigal

Erzulie

Freya

Hathor

Kali Ma

Mut

Oshun

Rhiannon

Shakti

Snake Woman

Tap Tun

Tashmetum

INDEPENDENCE

Aphrodite

Artemis

Baba Yaga

Dziewanna

Durga

Eostre

Gaia

Hathor

Hecate

Hera

Isis

Ista Devata

Ix Chel

Kali Ma

Lajja Gauri

Lilith

Medb

Rhiannon

Sarasvati

Shakti

Skadi

Snake Woman

Uni

INFERTILITY

Astarte

Juno

Mami Wata

Nephthys

Uttu

Vesna

INFIDELITY

Aphrodite

Blodeuwedd

Erzulie

Hathor

Hera

Juno

Oshun

Po Ino Nogar
Uni

INITIATION

Aida Wedo

Arianrhod

Artemis

Ceres

Cerridwen

Chalchiuhtlicue

Demeter

Eostre

Ereshkigal

Hathor

Ishtar

Isis

Izanami

Julunggul

Morrigu

Nanshe

Onatha

Persephone

Proserpina

Shakti

Shamhat

Snake Woman

INSPIRATION

Agemem

Boann

Branwen

Brigid

Calliope

Canola

Cerridwen

Coventina

Erzulie

Gunnlod

Hathor

Isis

Minerva

Oshun

Rhiannon

Saga

Sarasvati

Shakti

Shekinah

Yemaya

Yum Chenmo

INTUITIVE ABILITIES

Acpaxapo

Akonadi

Cerridwen

Corra

Gullveig

Hathor

Isis

Mami Wata

Minona

Morrigu

Nephthys

Ngame

Red Tara

Shakti

Shekinah

Snake Woman

Spider Woman

Sulis

INVENTIONS

Atargatis

Athene

Canola

Cerridwen

Isis

Minerva

Sarasvati

Shakti

Sura

JEALOUSY

Aphrodite

Artemis

Ereshkigal

The Erinyes

Erzulie

Kali Ma

Lamia

Morrigu

Shakti

JEWELRY

Aglaia

Amaterasu Omikami

Aphrodite

Brigid

Erzulie

Estsanatlehi

Freya

Hathor

Isis

Mami Wata

Mawu

Oshun

Parvati

Shakti

Yemaya

JUDGMENT

Artemis

Astraea

Badb

Calliope

Cerridwen

Dike

Ereshkigal

Gula

Hecate

Ishtar

Kali Ma

Ma'at

Morrigu

Nemesis

The Norns

Sekhmet

Sophia

The Valkyries

Var

JUSTICE

Akonadi

Astraea

Baba Yaga

Badb

Cerridwen

Dike

Ereshkigal

The Erinyes

Gula

Inanna

Izanami

Kali Ma

Ma'at

Morrigu

Nanshe

Nemesis

Ninlil

Sekhmet

Skadi

Themis

Var

KARMA

Akonadi

Ananke

Baba Yaga

Cerridwen

Ereshkigal

The Erinyes

Holda

Kali Ma

Kuan Yin

Lama

Nemesis

Shakti

Sophia

Vila

KNOWLEDGE

See WISDOM

LAW

Akonadi

Ala

Ananke

Astraea

Banba

Cerridwen

Dike

Ereshkigal

Ériu

Fódla

Inanna

Ma'at

Mami Wata

Mawu

Sekhmet

Shakti

Shekinah

Sigyn

Sophia

Themis

Var

LEARNING

Apakura

Baba Yaga

Benten

Branwen

Brigid

Cerridwen

Dana

Isis

Metis

Sarasvati

Shakti

Shamhat

LIFE

Amaterasu Omikami

Andraste

Arianrhod

Asase Yaa

Asherah

Ba Ngu'

Baba Yaga

Bugady Musun

Coatlicue

Cybele

Devi

Eka Abassi

Gula

Hathor

Isis

Lada

Lady of Beasts

Lama

Maia

Mawu

Maya

Medusa

Mokosh

Nammu

Nana Buluku

Ngame

Ninhursag

Ninti

The Norns

Parvati

Saule

Sedna

Shakti

Siduri Sabitu

Sophia

Ushas

Ved'Ma

Yemaya

Zywie

LIGHT

Aglaia

Aine

Amaterasu Omikami

Ararat

Astghik

Atthar

Aurora

Biliku

Bixia Yuanjin

Brigid

Bunzi

Candelifera

Eostre

Fravashi

Inanna

Iris

Isis

Kamui Fuchi

Lakshmi

Lucina

Ngame

Shakti

Shekinah

Tawaret

The Valkyries

Zaria

The Zorya

LONGEVITY

Anna Perenna

Artemis

Cerridwen

Ch'ang O

Coventina

Freya

Hecate

Holda

Hsi Wang Mu

Idunn

Isis

Julunggul

Mawu

Oenothea

Saule

Shakti

Siduri Sabitu

Skadi

White Tara

LOVE, ATTRACTING

Aine

Anath

Aphrodite

Artimpaasa

Astghik

Bast

Benten

Chuang Mu

Creddylad

Devi

Dzydzilelya

Eostre

Ereshkigal

Erzulie

Freya

Frigga

Hathor

Ishtar

Isis

Lada

Lakshmi

Lofn

Ma Gu

Mami Wata

Ningal

Oshun

Parvati

Psyche

Rati

Red Tara

Sarasvati

Shakti

Sjöfn

Tashmetum

Tlazolteotl

Venus

Xochiquetzal

Yaoji

Yemaya

LOVE, EMOTIONAL

Ananke

Artimpaasa

Astghik

Bast

Benten

Branwen

Creddylad

Devi

Dzydzilelya

Eostre

Erzulie

Faumea

Hi'iaka

Inanna

Isis

Kuan Yin

Lada

Lady of Beasts

Lakshmi

Lofn

Maia

Oba

Papatuanuku

Po Ino Nogar

Radha

Shakti

Sjöfn

Sophia

Tashmetum

Venus

Yaoji

Yemaya

LOVE, HEALING A BROKEN HEART

Artimpaasa

Astghik

Devi

Ereshkigal

Erzulie

Hera

Hestia

Kuan Yin

Lady of Beasts

Morrigu

Oba

Oshun

Papatuanuku

Parvati

Radha

Red Tara

Shakti

Sophia

Tlazolteotl

Uni

Venus

Yaoji

LOVE, PARENTAL

Akwaba

Ceres

Demeter

Enekpe

Erua

Faumea

Frigga

Kikimora

Matronae

Nana Buluku

Parvati

Shekinah

Tiamat

LOVE, ROMANTIC

Anath

Aphrodite

Artimpaasa

Astghik

Bast

Benten

Branwen

Ch'ang O

Chuang Mu

Creddylad

Devi

Dzydzilelya

Eostre

Erzulie

Freya

Ishtar

Isis

Juno

Lada

Lady of Beasts

Lofn

Ma Gu

Oshun

Papatuanuku

Psyche

Radha

Sarasvati

Shakti

Sjöfn

Tashmetum

Venus

Yaoji

Yemaya

LOVE, UNCONDITIONAL

Aine

Al-Uzza

Ananke

Andraste

Artimpaasa

Asherah

Astghik

Chalchiuhtlicue

Devi

Enekpe

Ereshkigal

Eurynome

Frigga

Hestia

Isis

Kali Ma

Kuan Yin

Lada

Lady of Beasts

Parvati

Psyche

Radha

Shakti

Shekinah

Sophia

Uni

Venus

Yaoji

LOYALTY

Ananke

Gula

Hera

Juno

Lajja Gauri

Lofn

Ningal

Parvati

Red Tara

Shekinah

Sigyn

Sita

Uni

The Valkyries

Venus

MAGICK, DARK

Artemis

Baba Yaga

Cerridwen

Circe

Ereshkigal

Hecate

Hina

Holda

Isis

Izanami

Kali Ma

Krtya

Lilith

Marama

Medusa

Morrigu

Nephthys

Onatha

Persephone

Proserpina

Rangda

Scathach

Shakti

Skadi

The Valkyries

MAGICK, LIGHT

Amaterasu Omikami

Aphrodite

Artemis

Atthar

Banba

Brigid

Cerridwen

Ch'ang O

Circe

Dana

Fravashi

Frigga

Gaia

Hina

Holda

Inanna

Isis

Kamrusepas

Krtya

Lilith

Morrigu

Nephthys

Onatha

Persephone

Proserpina

Red Tara

Rhiannon

Selene

Sól

Yemaya

MAGICK, LUNAR

Ararat

Arianrhod

Artemis

Artimpaasa

Astarte

Bast

Bendis

Cerridwen

Ch'ang O

Coatlicue

Coyolxauhqui

Diana

Dziewanna

Fravashi

Gleti

Hathor

Hecate

Hina

Ishtar

Isis

Ix Chel

Lilith

Lucina

Mama Quilla

Marama

Mawu

Morrigu

Odudua

Selene

Shakti

The Valkyries

Yemaya

Magick, solar

Aine

Akewa

Amaterasu Omikami

Atthar

Bast

Brigid

Chup Kamui

Estsanatlehi

Fravashi

Hathor

Hekit

Hina

Isis

Odudua

Sekhmet

Saule

Sól

The Valkyries

Wadjet

Xi Hou

The Zorya

Magickal Arts

Aine

Airmed

Andraste

Arianrhod

Baba Yaga

Badb

Banba

Brigid

Carmenta

Chun T'i

Coyolxauhqui

Demeter

Eir

Ereshkigal

Ériu

Fódla

Freya

Frigga

Haumea

Hecate

Hina

Inanna

Isis

Ix Chel

Kamrusepas

Krtya

Kupala

Macha

Maia

Maya

Morrigu

Nammu

Nana Buluku

Nephthys

Oya

Pasiphae

Rhiannon

Sarasvati

Sekhmet

Shakti

Sif

Sjöfn

Snake Woman

Sophia

Spider Woman

Tap Tun

The Valkyries

Ved'Ma

Yaoji

Yemaya

The Zorya

MANIFESTATION

Ananke

Aziri

Coventina

Danu

Eostre

Green Tara

Haltia

Kali Ma

Lada

Mara

Mati-Syra-Zemlya

Maya

Oba

Odudua

Radha

Red Tara

Shakti

Shekinah
Spider Woman
Tashmetum
Yellow Tara

MANIPULATION

Athene
Baba Yaga
Erzulie
Flidais
Hera
Inanna
Isis
Kali Ma
Rangda
Snake Woman
Uni
Uzume

MARIJUANA / HEMP

Bast
Circe
Ma Gu
Medb

MARRIAGE

Ananke
Bast
Chalchiuhtlicue

Dzydzilelya
Ereshkigal
Erua
Erzulie
Estsanatlehi
Frigga
Hathor
Hera
Indrani
Ishtar
Isis
Ix Chel
Juno
Lady of Beasts
Lajja Gauri
Lofn
Mama Quilla
Medb
Mokosh
Neith
Ninlil
Nu Kua
Oshun
Parvati
Psyche
Radha
Shakti
Shekinah
Sigyn
Sita

Sjöfn
Skadi
Sophia
Uni
Var
Venus
Xochiquetzal
The Zorya

MARTIAL ARTS

Brigid
Kali Ma
Scathach
The Valkyries

MATERIAL POSSESSIONS

Aziri
Chantico
Hathor
Inanna
Isis
Koevasi
Lajja Gauri
Lakshmi
Mami Wata
Rangda
Saule
Shakti
Yellow Tara

MEDITATION

Cerridwen
Green Tara
Kali Ma
Koliada
Kuan Yin
Shakti
Sheela Na Gig
White Tara
Yum Chenmo

MEMORY

Anna Perenna
Cerridwen
Isis
Meng-Po Niang Niang
Morrigu
Oya
Saga
Seshat
Shakti
Snake Woman

MEN

Apakura
Athene
Ceres
Ereshkigal
Hathor

Inanna
Isis
Julunggul
Kali Ma
Kunapipi
Lilith
Minerva
Morrigu
Mut
Neith
Nerthus
Pele
Seshat
Shakti
Shekinah
Tap Tun
The Valkyries

MENOPAUSE

Baba Yaga
Cerridwen
Ereshkigal
Estsanatlehi
Hecate
Kali Ma
Morrigu
Shakti
Sheela Na Gig
Yaya Zakurai

MENSES, FIRST

Artemis
Eostre
Estsanatlehi
Lajja Gauri
Lilith
Maia
Odudua
Shakti
Yaya Zakurai

MENSTRUATION

Ceres
Coyolxauhqui
Demeter
Estsanatlehi
Isis
Ix Chel
Kali Ma
Lakshmi
Mama Quilla
Medusa
Odudua
Rhea
Shakti
Sheela Na Gig
Snake Woman
Yaya Zakurai

MERCHANTS

Armathr

Aziri

Hera

Inari

Isis

Juno

Mara

Minerva

Nehallenia

Oya

Shakti

Uni

Yellow Tara

Yemaya

MERCY

Kuan Yin

Lakshmi

Ma'at

Saule

Shakti

Shekinah

Yemaya

METALWORKING

Athene

Brigid

Hina

Minerva

Xochiquetzal

MIRACLES

Cerridwen

Isis

Kuan Yin

Saule

Shakti

Shekinah

Sophia

MISCHIEF

Aphrodite

Baba Yaga

Badb

Baubo

Eostre

Freya

Kali Ma

Lilith

Medb

Morrigu

Venus

MONEY

Abundantia
Aje
Armathr
Ashiakle
Benten
Chantico
Copia
Habondia
Isis
Lakshmi
Mara
Ops
Oshun
Purandhi
Radha
Yellow Tara
Yemaya

MOON

Agemem
Ala
Al-Lat
Anna Perenna
Arianrhod
Artemis
Artimpaasa
Auchimalgen
Bast

Bendis
Branwen
Cerridwen
Ch'ang O
Chantico
Chup Kamui
Coatlicue
Coyolxauhqui
Diana
Dziewanna
Eurynome
Evaki
Freya
Gleti
Hathor
Hecate
Isis
Kali Ma
Leto
Lilith
Madre Vieja
Mama Quilla
Marama
Marzanna
Mawu
Morrigu
Ngame
Ningal
Pajau Yan
Pasiphae

Rhea

Rhiannon

Selene

Shakti

Tefnut

Tlazolteotl

Yemaya

The Zorya

MOTHERHOOD

Akwaba

Ala

Apakura

Artemis

Asase Yaa

Asherah

Astarte

Bachué

Bast

Brigid

Ceres

Chihucoatl

Chomo-Lung-Ma

Coatlicue

Cybele

Dana

Demeter

Devi

Diana

Eka Abassi

Epona

Eurynome

Frigga

Gaia

Hathor

Haumea

Hebat

Hecate

Hera

Hsi Wang Mu

Ishtar

Isis

Juno

Kali Ma

Kuan Yin

Lajja Gauri

Leto

Maia

Mama Oello

Mati-Syra-Zemlya

Matronae

Mawu

Mboze

Meskhenet

Mut

Nana Buluku

Nantosuelta

Nekhebet

Ninhursag

Ninsun

Nuneh

Nut

Oshun

Papatuanuku

Renenet

Rhea

Saule

Sekhmet

Selene

Shakti

Sheela Na Gig

Sophia

Spider Woman

Tawaret

Teteoinnan

Thalassa

Tozi

Uni

Vesta

Yemaya

Yum Chenmo

Mountains

Ararat

Artemis

Astarte

Britomartis

Cailleach

Chomo-Lung-Ma

Cybele

Diana

Durga

Gaia

Lady of Beasts

Mahuika

Maia

Ninhursag

Pachamama

Parvati

Pele

Satine

Shakti

Skadi

Tlalteuctli

Yama No Kami

Yaoji

Music

Aphrodite

Athene

Bast

Benten

Calliope

Canola

Cybele

Erzulie

Estsanatlehi

Freya

Hathor

Kipu-Tytto

Minerva

Oshun

Sarasvati

Shakti

Sjöfn

Uzume

Yemaya

Mysteries

Ananke

Arinna

Baba Yaga

Badb

Cerridwen

Chicomecoatl

Cybele

Diana

Don

Ereshkigal

Faumea

Frigga

Gaia

Hecate

Isis

Kali Ma

Lajja Gauri

Lakshmi

Lilith

Macha

Medusa

Momu

Morrigu

Ningal

Nut

Shakti

Shamhat

Sheela Na Gig

Shekinah

Snake Woman

Sophia

Tiamat

White Buffalo Calf Woman

Yaoji

The Zorya

Nature

Akwaba

Anuket

Asase Yaa

Ashnan

The Bereginy

Blodeuwedd

Britomartis

Ceres

Chomo-Lung-Ma

Coatlicue

Cybele

Dana

Demeter

Eostre

Estsanatlehi

Eurynome

Fravashi

Gaia

Hathor

Hecate

Hina

Jord

Kali Ma

Lajja Gauri

Leshachikha

Ma Gu

Mati-Syra-Zemlya

Matronae

Mawu

Mielikki

Nantosuelta

Nerthus

Onatha

Persephone

Pomona

Spider Woman

Tlalteuctli

Tozi

White Buffalo Calf Woman

The Zorya

NEGATIVE HABITS, TO OVERCOME

Anath

Baba Yaga

Blodeuwedd

Cerridwen

Fravashi

Indrani

Isis

Ix Chel

Kali Ma

Kuan Yin

Lilith

Morrigu

Nemesis

Shakti

Shekinah

Tlazolteotl

NIGHT

Ananke

Baba Yaga

Bendis

Cailleach

Cerridwen

Ereshkigal

Evaki
Frigga
Hecate
Hina
Ishtar
Isis
Kali Ma
Lilith
Manat
Manea
Marzanna
Morrigu
Nut
Shakti
Sheela Na Gig
Snake Woman
The Valkyries
The Zorya

Nourishment

Aha Njoku
Alemona
Amashilamma
Amaterasu Omikami
Annapatni
Asherah
Ashnan
Axomama
Carna

Chicomecoatl
Coatlicue
Copia
Corn Woman
Dewi Nawang Sasih
Dugnai
Gaia
Gyhldeptis
Habondia
Hebat
Hestia
Inari
Lajja Gauri
Lupa
Mama Allpa
Mayahuel
Mielikki
Mokosh
Mujaji
Ops
Pachamama
Parvati
Pax
Pomona
Renenet
Sangiyan Sari
Shakti
Sulis
Tawaret
Zaramama

OATHS

Ala

Al-Lat

Angerona

Artemis

Badb

Banba

Cerridwen

Ereshkigal

Ériu

Fódla

Hecate

Hera

Iris

Lilith

Morrigu

Nu Kua

Shakti

Shekinah

Themis

Uni

Var

White Tara

OBEDIENCE

Ananke

Gaia

Hera

Juno

Lajja Gauri

Matronae

Shekinah

Uni

OBSTACLES, TO REMOVE

Baba Yaga

Badb

Black Tara

Blue Tara

Carmenta

Cerridwen

Ereshkigal

Green Tara

Hecate

Indrani

Isis

Ix Chel

Juno

Kali Ma

Kuan Yin

Lakshmi

Lilith

Mami Wata

Matronae

Maya

Nehallenia

Onatha

Oshun

Parvati

Persephone

Proserpina

Psyche

Rhiannon

Shakti

Sigyn

Sheela Na Gig

Shekinah

Tlazolteotl

Uni

White Tara

Oceans, Rivers, and Bodies of Water

Anahit

Anna Perenna

Anuket

Aphrodite

Arianrhod

Arnamentia

Asherah

Ashiakle

Astghik

Atargatis

Ba Ngu'

Benten

Boann

Branwen

Chalchiuhtlicue

Coventina

Creddylad

Dana

Danu

Don

Erzulie

Eurynome

Faumea

Freya

Hecate

Hine

Holda

Ilmatar

Iris

Isis

Kupala

Lajja Gauri

Mama Cocha

Mami Wata

Mamlambo

Marica

Matsu

Mokosh

Momu

Morrigu

Mulhalmoni

Nammu

Nanshe

Nantosuelta
Nehallenia
Nu Kua
Oba
Oshun
Oya
Rán
Saranyu
Sarasvati
Sedna
Shakti
Sulis
Tawaret
Tefnut
Thalassa
Tiamat
Tlalteuctli
Tsovinar
Uzume
Vellamo
Venus
Yemaya

OPPORTUNITIES

Athene
Cerridwen
Isis
Kali Ma
Lakshmi

Shakti
Venus

ORDER

Ananke
Athene
Demeter
Dike
Estsanatlehi
Eurynome
Fravashi
Juno
Lada
Lilith
Nu Kua
Nut
Sekhmet
Shakti
The Valkyries
The Zorya

PASSION, LUST

Aine
Amaterasu Omikami
Ananke
Anath
Anuket
Aphrodite
Arianrhod

Astarte

Astghik

Baubo

Blodeuwedd

Chuang Mu

Cocomama

Creddylad

Dzydzilelya

Eostre

Ereshkigal

Erzulie

Eurynome

Flidais

Freya

Hathor

Ilmatar

Ishtar

Isis

Kali Ma

Lada

Lajja Gauri

Lilith

Lofn

Mami Wata

Medb

Odudua

Oshun

Parvati

Pasiphae

Pele

Radha

Rangda

Rati

Red Tara

Rhea

Sekhmet

Shakti

Shamhat

Sheela Na Gig

Sjöfn

Skadi

Tap Tun

Tlazolteotl

Venus

White Tara

PATRONESS OF THE HEALER

Brigid

Carna

Eir

Gula

Hekit

Ix Chel

Kamrusepas

Kuan Yin

Minerva

Mulhalmoni

Sekhmet

Shakti

Shekinah

Teteoinnan

Tozi

PATRONESS
OF THE PRIESTESS

Artemis

Brigid

Epona

Erzulie

Hathor

Hecate

Ishtar

Isis

Kuan Yin

Lilith

Mami Wata

Morrigu

Nephthys

Oshun

Shakti

Shamhat

Shekinah

Snake Woman

PATRONESS
OF THE WITCH

Arianrhod

Baba Yaga

Cerridwen

Gullveig

Hecate

Kali Ma

Krtya

Lilith

Maya

Medusa

Minona

Morrigu

Oya

Rangda

Shakti

Sheela Na Gig

Tlazolteotl

Yemaya

PEACE

Bast

Demeter

Durga

Erce

Hestia

Nerthus

Pax

Rhea
Shakti
Shekinah
Sif

PERFUME

Aphrodite
Bast
Cocomama
Erzulie
Hathor
Inanna
Isis
Lakshmi
Mami Wata
Oshun
Shakti
Shamhat
Venus
Yemaya

PHYSICAL LABOR

Carna
Elli
Mokosh
Ops
Tlalteuctli

PLEASURE

Aine
Ananke
Anath
Aphrodite
Astarte
Astghik
Bast
Baubo
Chantico
Chuang Mu
Cocomama
Erzulie
Eurynome
Freya
Frigga
Hathor
Ilmatar
Inanna
Ishtar
Isis
Kali Ma
Lada
Lajja Gauri
Lakshmi
Lilith
Lofn
Mami Wata
Medb

Morrigu

Odudua

Radha

Rati

Sekhmet

Shakti

Shamhat

Sheela Na Gig

Snake Woman

Uzume

Venus

Xochiquetzal

POETRY

Aine

Arianrhod

Benten

Blodeuwedd

Boann

Brigid

Calliope

Cerridwen

Devi

Eostre

Ereshkigal

Freya

Gunnlod

Hathor

Hecate

Idunn

Isis

Kali Ma

Kuan Yin

Morrigu

Rati

Saga

Tashmetum

Thalia

Ushas

Vac

POWER

Al-Uzza

Ananke

Baba Yaga

Baubo

Bia

Black Tara

Cailleach

Cerridwen

Durga

Ereshkigal

Flidais

Fódla

Green Tara

Hera

Isis

Juno

Kali Ma
Lakshmi
Lilith
Medb
Morrigu
Ninlil
Ninsun
Rhea
Sekhmet
Shakti
Shekinah
Snake Woman
Sól
Uni
Yemaya

PRAYER

Angerona
Brigid
Ch'ang O
Coatlicue
Estsanatlehi
Gaia
Kali Ma
Kuan Yin
Ninsun
Shakti
Shekinah
Tashmetum

Ushas
Vac
White Tara

PROBLEM SOLVING

Baba Yaga
Branwen
Ereshkigal
Fravashi
Isis
Mami Wata
Psyche
Shakti
Shekinah
Sophia
White Tara

PROPHECY

Acpaxapo
Akonadi
Ananke
Antevorta
Arianrhod
Auchimalgen
Baba Yaga
Brigid
Carmenta
Cerridwen
Corra

Coventina
Ereshkigal
Freya
Frigga
Gullveig
Hecate
Isis
Kuan Yin
Meskhenet
Morrigu
Nanshe
The Norns
Scathach
Shakti
Shekinah
Sif
Snake Woman
Spider Woman
Themis
The Valkyries
The Zorya

PROSPERITY

Abundantia
Aje
Anuket
Armathr
Ashiakle
Aziri

Ceres
Chantico
Cocomama
Copia
Dana
Demeter
Epona
Erzulie
Fortuna
Gullveig
Habondia
Hathor
Hecate
Inanna
Inari
Isis
Kuan Yin
Lajja Gauri
Lakshmi
Nehallenia
Ops
Oshun
Pax
Purandhi
Radha
Sarasvati
Shakti
Shekinah
Sita
Tyche

Vasudhara

Yellow Tara

PROTECTION

Alemona

Angerona

Anuket

Apakura

Arinna

Artemis

Athene

Auchimalgen

Ba Ngu'

Bast

Black Tara

Blue Tara

Britomartis

Bugady Musun

Caipora

Candelifera

Carmenta

Ceres

Cerridwen

Chantico

Chasca

Coatlicue

Demeter

Devi

Druantia

Durga

Ereshkigal

Eurynome

Flidais

Freya

Frigga

Haltia

Hathor

Hecate

Hera

Inanna

Ishtar

Isis

Juno

Kali Ma

Kamui Fuchi

Kuan Yin

Lajja Gauri

Lama

Leshachikha

Lilith

Lupa

Mati-Syra-Zemlya

Matronae

Matsu

Meskhenet

Mielikki

Minona

Morrigu

Nana Buluku

Nantosuelta

Nehallenia

Neith

Nekhebet

Nephthys

Nuneh

Nut

Oba

Oya

Rhea

Samovila

Saule

Sekhmet

Sengdroma

Shakti

Shasti

Sheela Na Gig

Shekinah

Sophia

Tawaret

Teteoinnan

Uni

The Valkyries

Vila

Wadjet

Yama No Kami

Yemaya

The Zorya

PSYCHIC ABILITIES

Acpaxapo

Cerridwen

Gullveig

Hecate

Isis

Izanami

Minona

The Norns

Pele

Scathach

Shakti

Snake Woman

Teteoinnan

Vac

The Valkyries

PUBERTY

Akwaba

Apakura

Artemis

Baba Yaga

Eostre

Green Tara

Gunnlod

Hera

Idunn

Julunggul

Kunapipi

Lajja Gauri
Onatha
Persephone
Proserpina
Radha
Rati
Shakti
Shamhat
Uni
Zaria

Public Speaking

Brigid
Calliope
Itzpapalotl
Koevasi
Minerva
Saga
Sarasvati
Vac

Purification

Arnamentia
Aryong Jong
Astraea
Chalchiuhtlicue
Ch'ang O
Chihucoatl
Coatlicue

Green Tara
Hecate
Isis
Itzpapalotl
Kuan Yin
Kunapipi
Kupala
Lakshmi
Momu
Parvati
Sedna
Shakti
Shekinah
Shitala
Sulis
Tlazolteotl
Tozi
Venus
Vila
Xi Hou
Yemaya
Zaria

Rape, healing from

Aine
Artemis
Artimpaasa
Athene
Chuang Mu

Hera

Matronae

Ninlil

Rati

Sekhmet

Shekinah

Sita

Sulis

Uni

Venus

Wakahirume

Xochiquetzal

REBIRTH

Airmed

Anapel

Asase Yaa

Baba Yaga

Badb

Candelifera

Ceres

Cerridwen

Chalchiuhtlicue

Coatlicue

Cybele

Demeter

Eostre

Estsanatlehi

Hestia

Idunn

Inanna

Isis

Ix Chel

Izanami

Julunggul

Koliada

Lakshmi

Leshachikha

Lilith

Mahuika

Mami Wata

Medusa

Meskhenet

Nekhebet

Nephthys

Ninti

Nut

Onatha

Persephone

Proserpina

Shakti

Shekinah

Tiamat

The Valkyries

Yemaya

The Zorya

Zywie

REGENERATION

Anath

Atthar

Ceres

Cerridwen

Demeter

Eostre

Estsanatlehi

Hathor

Hecate

Idunn

Ishtar

Isis

Ix Chel

Kali Ma

Mama Quilla

Morrigu

Oba

Saule

Shakti

Shamhat

Zywie

REINCARNATION

Anapel

Badb

Cerridwen

Hecate

Kali Ma

Kamui Fuchi

Kuan Yin

Mawu

Meng-Po Niang Niang

Nut

Shakti

RENEWING

Airmed

Anna Perenna

Arianrhod

Aurora

Badb

Ceres

Cerridwen

Corn Woman

Coventina

Demeter

Eostre

Hathor

Hecate

Idunn

Isis

Koliada

Leshachikha

Marzanna

Mawu

Minerva

Shakti

Tlazolteotl

RESURRECTION

Eir

Eostre

Frigga

Hi'iaka

Inanna

Isis

Marzanna

Nanshe

Nephthys

Nut

RETRIBUTION

Aine

Aphrodite

Arianrhod

Artemis

Baba Yaga

Black Tara

Ceres

Cerridwen

Demeter

Ereshkigal

The Erinyes

Gula

Hi'iaka

Hsi Wang Mu

Ishtar

Isis

Izanami

Kali Ma

Mahuika

Medb

Morrigu

Nemesis

Oba

The Valkyries

RITUALS AND CEREMONIES

Atargatis

Bona Dea

Brogla

Cerridwen

Corn Woman

Cybele

Durga

The Erinyes

Ertha

Estsanatlehi

Gula

Hecate

Ishtar

Isis

Kali Ma

Kamrusepas
Mama Quilla
Marzanna
Medusa
Nephthys
Samovila
Seshat
Shakti
Shamhat
Tlazolteotl
White Buffalo Calf Woman
Yama No Kami

SACRIFICE

Badb
Enekpe
Itzpapalotl
Ixtab
Psyche
Sigyn
Sita

SCIENCES / ALCHEMY

Ananke
Cerridwen
Ereshkigal
Hathor
Hecate

Isis
Kuan Yin
Minerva
Ninhursag
Sarasvati
Seshat
Shakti
The Zorya

SEASONS

Al-Uzza
Cailleach
Cerridwen
Demeter
Dike
Eostre
Estsanatlehi
Hecate
Onatha
Persephone
Shakti
Yama No Kami
The Zorya

SECRETS

Frigga
Gullveig
Krtya

Marzanna

Sigyn

Yaoji

SEDUCTION

Aphrodite

Astarte

Bast

Cocomama

Erzulie

Freya

Frigga

Hathor

Ishtar

Lilith

Lofn

Mami Wata

Odudua

Oshun

Rangda

Rati

Red Tara

Shamhat

Sjöfn

Tap Tun

Venus

SELF-GROWTH

Artemis

Asase Yaa

Baba Yaga

Baubo

Ceres

Eostre

Estsanatlehi

Green Tara

Isis

Ista Devata

Kupala

Lama

Mami Wata

Matsu

Nammu

Oya

Po Ino Nogar

Psyche

Rhiannon

Shakti

Shekinah

Uzume

SELF-IMAGE

Aglaia

Baubo

Ista Devata

Medusa

Psyche

Sgeg Mo Ma

Shekinah

Venus

Yaya Zakurai

SENSUALITY

Amaterasu Omikami

Anath

Aphrodite

Artimpaasa

Astghik

Bast

Baubo

Chuang Mu

Cocomama

Creddylad

Eostre

Ereshkigal

Erzulie

Flora

Freya

Hathor

Ilmatar

Ishtar

Isis

Kali Ma

Lajja Gauri

Lilith

Ma Gu

Medb

Oshun

Parvati

Rati

Sarasvati

Shakti

Shamhat

Sheela Na Gig

Venus

Vesna

Xochiquetzal

Yaya Zakurai

SEXUALITY AND SEXUAL ACTIVITIES

Anahit

Ananke

Anath

Aphrodite

Astarte

Bast

Chuang Mu

Cocomama

Cybele

Druantia

Dzydzilelya

Eostre

Ereshkigal

Erzulie

Estsanatlehi

Faumea

Flidais

Flora

Freya

Frigga

Hathor

Ilmatar

Inanna

Ishtar

Isis

Ista Devata

Ix Chel

Kali Ma

Kupala

Lilith

Lupa

Maia

Mami Wata

Medusa

Odudua

Oshun

Rangda

Rati

Red Tara

Rhea

Scathach

Shakti

Shamhat

Sjöfn

Snake Woman

Tap Tun

Tlazolteotl

Xochiquetzal

Venus

Vesna

White Buffalo Calf Woman

Yaya Zakurai

SHAMANISM

Artio

Eir

Etugen

Hel

Inanna

Itzpapalotl

Mama Cocha

Mulhalmoni

Ninhursag

Saga

Uzume

Yondung Halmoni

SHAPESHIFTING

Artemis

Baba Yaga

Cerridwen

Diana

Eostre

Ereshkigal

Flidais

Haumea

Hecate

Inari

Isis

Kali

Marica

Maya

Morrigu

Oshun

Oya

Parvati

Samovila

Shakti

The Valkyries

Vila

Sisterhood

Akewa

Artemis

Athene

Banba

Brigid

Diana

Ereshkigal

Ériu

Fódla

Hecate

Inanna

Ishtar

Isis

Lilith

The Mar'rallang

Medusa

Nephthys

Shakti

Snake Woman

The Valkyries

Sky

Al-Uzza

Ananke

Arianrhod

Ausrine

Beiwe

Bixia Yuanjin

Cerridwen

Coatlicue

Don

Ereshkigal

Eurynome

Frigga

Hathor

Hebat

Hecate

Holda

Ilmatar

Inanna

Iris

Ishtar

Isis

Izanami

Kali Ma

Lajja Gauri

Nu Kua

Nut

Sedna

Shakti

Ushas

The Valkyries

The Zorya

SLEEP

Chuang Mu

Ereshkigal

Evaki

Iris

Kikimora

Nirriti

Nut

Selene

Shakti

The Zorya

SORCERESS

Arianrhod

Baba Yaga

Cerridwen

Chun T'i

Circe

Dana

Devi

Diana

Ereshkigal

Gullveig

Haumea

Hecate

Isis

Krtya

Kupala

Lilith

Malinalxochitl

Marica

Minona

Morrigu

Oya

Red Tara

Sedna

Sheela Na Gig

Snake Woman

Yaoji

SPELLCASTING

Arianrhod

Baba Yaga

Cailleach

Carmenta

Cerridwen

Circe

Ereshkigal

Erzulie

Gullveig

Hecate

Holda

Isis

Kamrusepas

Krtya

Lilith

Marica

Morrigu

Oshun

Pasiphae

Rangda

Red Tara

Sif

Tiamat

SPELLCASTING, TO BREAK A SPELL

Baba Yaga

Cerridwen

Circe

Erzulie

Gullveig

Hecate

Holda

Isis

Kamrusepas

Krtya

Marica

Morrigu

Rangda

Red Tara

Sif

SPIRITS / GHOSTS

Auchimalgen

Black Tara

Ereshkigal

Hecate

Hel

Holda

Iris

Ixtab

Mami Wata

Manea

Morrigu

Nephthys

Nut

Oya

Pajau Yan

Pinga

Rán

Red Tara

Satine

Saule

Sheela Na Gig

Skadi

Themis

Tuonetar

The Valkyries

Zywie

Spiritual Connection/ Illumination

Aida Wedo

Akewa

Angerona

Asherah

Boann

Cerridwen

Coatlicue

Devi

Fravashi

Hine

Iris

Kali Ma

Kuan Yin

Lakshmi

Lamia

Lucina

The Mar'rallang

Maya

Ngame

Red Tara

Shakti

Shekinah

Snake Woman

Sophia

Spider Woman

Tozi

Ushas

Vasudhara

Spirituality

Ananke

Asherah

Black Tara

Blue Tara

Devi

Eir

Fravashi

Green Tara

Kuan Yin

Kupala
Lakshmi
Mami Wata
Mawu
Maya
Ninlil
Pachamama
Red Tara
Shakti
Shamhat
Sheela Na Gig
Shekinah
Snake Woman
Sophia
Tozi
Ushas
White Tara
Yaoji
Yellow Tara

SPORTS

See ATHLETICS

STORMS

Baduhenna
Bardaichila
Biliku
Cerridwen

Hecate
Ix Chel
Kali Ma
Lilith
Matsu
Oya
Rán
Shakti
Tsovinar
Ved'Ma
Yuki Onne

STRENGTH, PHYSICAL

Atthar
Bia
Branwen
Carna
Diana
Elli
Faumea
Idunn
Lady of Beasts
Rangda
Shakti
Sól
White Tara

STUDENTS AND STUDYING

Dana

Isis

Juno

Minerva

Saga

Sarasvati

Seshat

Shakti

Spider Woman

SUCCESS

Abundantia

Athene

Fravashi

Hathor

Isis

Kuan Yin

Lakshmi

Nike

Oya

Psyche

Shakti

Tyche

SUN

Agemem

Aine

Akewa

Al-Lat

Amaterasu Omikami

Ararat

Arinna

Atthar

Bast

Beiwe

Chup Kamui

Evaki

Hathor

Hebat

Hekit

Hina

Isis

Kali Ma

Kuan Yin

Lajja Gauri

Leto

Mut

Pasiphae

Saule

Shakti

Sól

Sulis

Tefnut

Wadjet

Xi Hou

The Zorya

TAROT

Cerridwen

Hathor

Hecate

Minerva

TEMPERANCE

Kuan Yin

Lakshmi

Oba

Psyche

Rhiannon

Shakti

Shekinah

Sita

Sól

Tlazolteotl

THIEVERY

Baba Yaga

Ch'ang O

Evaki

Hecate

Nirriti

Rhiannon

TIME

Al-Uzza

Ananke

Anna Perenna

Arianrhod

Baba Yaga

Cerridwen

Coventina

Coyolxauhqui

Druantia

Ereshkigal

Estsanatlehi

Gaia

Hecate

Koliada

Hine

Kali Ma

Lajja Gauri

Mama Quilla

Medusa

Nut

Oba

Rhea

Sarasvati

Shakti

Shekinah

The Valkyries

The Zorya

TRANSFORMATION

Aida Wedo

Aspelenie

Baba Yaga

Blodeuwedd

Blue Tara

Cailleach

Cerridwen

Danu

Demeter

Eostre

Estsanatlehi

Gyhldeptis

Hecate

Hina

Itzpapalotl

Julunggul

Kali Ma

Kamrusepas

Koevasi

Kunapipi

Mahuika

Malinalxochitl

Marica

Maya

Medusa

Odudua

Onatha

Oya

Parvati

Pele

Persephone

Proserpina

Psyche

Shakti

Shamhat

Sheela Na Gig

Shekinah

Tabiti

Vila

Yemaya

TRAVEL

Al-Uzza

Artemis

Ba Ngu'

Feronia

Hecate

Hine

Iris

Isis

Nehallenia

Yemaya

TREASURES, HIDDEN

Aida Wedo

Aphrodite

Baba Yaga

Chantico

Eostre

Erzulie

Fortuna

Isis

Mama Cocha

Oya

Pele

Sarasvati

Sedna

Shakti

Yemaya

TRUTH

Asase Yaa

Astraea

Atthar

Baba Yaga

Cerridwen

Ereshkigal

Hecate

Isis

Kali Ma

Kuan Yin

Lajja Gauri

Ma'at

Marzanna

Maya

Medusa

Minerva

Nemesis

Radha

Renenet

Rhiannon

Sekhmet

Sgeg Mo Ma

Shakti

Shekinah

Themis

Ushas

Vac

White Buffalo Calf Woman

White Tara

The Zorya

THE UNDERWORLD

Ala

Black Tara

Cailleach

Cerridwen

Don

Ereshkigal

Gula

Hecate

Hecate

Hel

Hine

Izanami

Lada

Mahuika

Manea

Medusa

Meng-Po Niang Niang

Nephthys

Ninlil

Nut

Onatha

Oya

Persephone

Proserpina

Rhiannon

Satine

Sedna

Skadi

Sophia

Tuonetar

The Valkyries

VEGETATION

The Bereginy

Brigid

Ceres

Chalchiuhtlicue

Corn Woman

Demeter

Druantia

Eostre

Erce

Etugen

Flora

Fravashi

Gaia

Gyhldeptis

Hathor

Haumea

Isis

Jord

Kunapipi

Kupala

Lady of Beasts

Ma Gu

Marica

Mayahuel

Ninhursag

Onatha

Pachamama

Pani

Pele

Persephone

Pomona

Proserpina

Rhea

Samovila

Shakti

Spider Woman

Tlalteuctli

Venus

Vila

Xochiquetzal

Yama No Kami

Yaya Zakurai

Vengeance, Revenge

Anath

Apakura

Aphrodite

Artemis

Athene

Cerridwen

Coyolxauhqui

The Erinyes

Erzulie

Gula

Hecate

Hera

Hi'iaka

Indrani

Ishtar

Isis

Kali Ma

Lamia

Morrigu

Nemesis

Ninlil

Pele

Persephone

Proserpina

Skadi

Sulis

Tiamat

Uni

The Valkyries

Var

Vila

Victory

Anath

Andraste

Astarte

Athene

Badb

Baduhenna

Banba

Black Tara

Brigantia

Durga

Ereshkigal

Ériu

Fódla

Hathor

Hecate

Inanna

Iris

Ishtar

Isis

Kali Ma

Neith

Nike

Psyche

Shakti

Shekinah

Sigyn

The Valkyries

Venus

The Zorya

VIOLENCE

Artemis

Badb

Bia

Cerridwen

Chantico

Ereshkigal

Frigga

Hera

Inanna

Ishtar

Kali Ma

Medb

Morrigu

Pele

Sekhmet

Tiamat

Uni

The Valkyries

WAR AND BATTLES

Anahit

Anath

Andraste

Aphrodite

Arinna

Artemis

Astarte

Athene

Badb

Baduhenna

Black Tara

Chihucoatl

Chun T'i

Dana

Durga

Ereshkigal

Freya

Hebat

Hecate

Hine

Inanna

Ishtar

Kali Ma

Macha

Medb

Morrigu

Neith

Nekhebet

Nike

Sekhmet

Sophia

Tefnut

The Valkyries

Venus

Macha

Medb

Medusa

Minerva

Morrigu

Neith

Scathach

Sekhmet

Tiamat

The Valkyries

The Zorya

WARRIOR GODDESSES

Al-Uzza

Anath

Andraste

Apakura

Aphrodite

Astarte

Athene

Badb

Brigid

Chihucoatl

Chun T'i

Durga

Ereshkigal

Inanna

Ishtar

Isis

Kali Ma

WEALTH

Abundantia

Aida Wedo

Aje

Ashiakle

Aziri

Benten

Chantico

Copia

Erzulie

Fortuna

Freya

Habondia

Hecate

Hestia

Inanna

Ishtar

Isis

Lajja Gauri

Lakshmi

Mami Wata

Mamlambo

Nerthus

Ops

Oshun

Pax

Purandhi

Radha

Saule

Shakti

Sif

Vasudhara

Yellow Tara

Yemaya

WEAPONS

Artemis

Athene

Badb

Durga

Ereshkigal

Hecate

Inanna

Ishtar

Kali Ma

Minerva

Neith

Scathach

The Valkyries

WEATHER

Artemis

Aryong Jong

Baba Yaga

Brogla

Bunzi

Cailleach

Cerridwen

Dziewanna

Hecate

Holda

Ix Chel

Julunggul

Lilith

Marzanna

Mbaba Mwana Waresa

Mboze

Mujaji

Oya

Tefnut

Yondung Halmoni

WEAVING AND SPINNING

Aida Wedo

Amaterasu Omikami

Arachne

Arianrhod

Athene

Demeter

Frigga

Isis

Ix Chel

Kikimora

Leto

Mama Oello

Mara

Maya

Minona

Mokosh

Neith

Pukkeenegak

Shakti

Spider Woman

Uttu

Wakahirume

Xochiquetzal

WEIGHT LOSS

Annapatni

Ashnan

Atthar

Bia

Branwen

Carna

Cerridwen

Ch'ang O

Diana

Elli

Faumea

Hathor

Idunn

Isis

Lady of Beasts

Rangda

Sangiyan Sari

Shakti

Sól

Sulis

White Tara

WHOLENESS

Aida Wedo

Ch'ang O

Gyhldeptis

Hestia

Hina

Izanami

Kuan Yin

The Mar'rallang

Matsu

Ningal

Pachamama

Psyche

Shakti

Shekinah

Sulis

Yemaya

WINE

Asherah

Bona Dea

Flora

Hathor

Isis

Ma Gu

Mayahuel

Mati-Syra-Zemlya

Mbaba Mwana Waresa

Ninkasi

Nut

Oenothea

Oya

Pereplut

Persephone

Proserpina

Shakti

Siduri Sabitu

Sura

Vesna

WISDOM

Ananke

Arianrhod

Artemis

Asherah

Athene

Baba Yaga

Benten

Black Tara

Blodeuwedd

Blue Tara

Brigid

Cailleach

Cerridwen

Corra

Dana

Druantia

Ereshkigal

Frigga

Green Tara

Hecate

Holda

Isis

Kali Ma

Kamui Fuchi

Lilith
Lupa
Ma'at
Mati-Syra-Zemlya
Mawu
Maya
Medusa
Metis
Minerva
Minona
Morrigu
Nammu
Nana Buluku
Ninsun
Nuneh
Red Tara
Sarasvati
Seshat
Shakti
Shekinah
Siduri Sabitu
Skadi
Snake Woman
Sophia
Spider Woman
Sulis
Tashmetum
Ushas
White Tara
Yellow Tara

Yemaya
Yum Chenmo
The Zorya

WITCHCRAFT

Airmed
Baba Yaga
Brigid
Cerridwen
Circe
Ereshkigal
Erzulie
Feronia
Freya
Gullveig
Hecate
Holda
Isis
Krtya
Kupala
Lilith
Marica
Medusa
Minona
Morrigu
Pasiphae
Rangda
Tlazolteotl
Yemaya

WOMEN AND FEMININITY

Aha Njoku

Akewa

Ala

Aphrodite

Arianrhod

Artemis

Asherah

Athene

Bast

Benten

The Bereginy

Bona Dea

Brigid

Ceres

Cerridwen

Ch'ang O

Chicomecoatl

Coatlicue

Cybele

Devi

Dewi Nawang Sasih

Diana

Eir

Erzulie

Freya

Gaia

Hathor

Hecate

Hera

Hina

Hine

Iris

Isis

Ix Chel

Juno

Kuan Yin

Lilith

Macha

Mama Quilla

Medusa

Minerva

Minona

Mokosh

Morrigu

Neith

Nekhebet

Ningal

Nirriti

Oshun

Pachamama

Renenet

Shakti

Sheela Na Gig

Shekinah

Snake Woman

Teteoinnan

Uni

Ushas

Venus

Xochiquetzal

Yama No Kami

Yemaya

WOODLANDS AND FORESTS

Aja

Andraste

Ardwinna

Artemis

Asherah

Athene

Atira

Baba Yaga

Baduhenna

The Bereginy

Blodeuwedd

Caipora

Cerridwen

Creddylad

Cybele

Demeter

Diana

Druantia

Dziewanna

Eostre

Etugen

Feronia

Flidais

Gaia

Gyhldeptis

Haumea

Hecate

Hi'iaka

Jord

Leshachikha

Marica

Medb

Mielikki

Minona

Nerthus

Onatha

Pachamama

Papatuanuku

Persephone

Pomona

Proserpina

Shakti

Skadi

Tabiti

Vesna

Vila

Yama No Kami

WRITING

Athene

Benten

Brigid

Calliope

Cerridwen

Freya

Hathor

Idunn

Minerva

Saga

Sarasvati

Seshat

Tashmetum

Thalia

Ushas

Yum Chenmo

YOUTH

Anath

Aphrodite

Artemis

Branwen

Britomartis

Creddylad

Eostre

Gunnlod

Hathor

Hestia

Idunn

Ix Chel

Kupala

Lada

Lajja Gauri

Maia

Maya

Shakti

Ved'Ma

Venus

Vesna

Wakahirume

White Tara

Yaya Zakurai

THREE

· · · · · · · · · · · ✳ · · · · · · · · · · ·

Color Rays

Color is simply a form of light holding a vibration, the only energy source visible to the human eye. Every color has its own purpose, its own level of power and holiness. An attraction or aversion to a particular shade can say much about who we are and the healing we need to receive. Our affinity to certain hues can also lead us to many different aspects of the Goddess. For example, you may have recently become attracted to orange and brown hues, with these colors making new appearances in your wardrobe and home decorating. By knowing which goddess considers orange and brown sacred, you will know which aspect of the Goddess is becoming apparent in your life, influencing your day-to-day energy.

The use of color in ceremonial altars and spellwork is essential to the success of a rite. Using hues sacred to a goddess, you can easily express your intention and pay tribute to her in a ritualistic way.

Red: Sensuality, sex, passion, energy, willpower, anger, transformation, manifestation, war, battles, elemental fire, determination, independence, masculinity, physical strength, aggression, courage, physical healing, the hearth, power, wild woman instincts, the warrior instinct.

Orange: Sexual potency, material and physical desires, self-integration, warmth, attraction, celebrations, business success, stimulation, birthing new ideas, abundance, optimism, wisdom, weakness into strength.

Yellow: Intellect, wisdom, learning, knowledge, study, mental clarity, spiritual surrender, eliminating negativity, happiness, joy, cheerfulness, self-knowledge, confidence, vitality, energy, elemental air, springtime, fertility, artistic endeavors, magick, travel, progress in worldly and spiritual affairs, speaking, writing.

Green: Abundance, prosperity, material blessings, Earth Mother, nature, harvest, elemental earth, fertility, growth, silence, calm, knowledge, harmony, balance, recovering, healing, peace, hope, plants and herbs, earth magick, home, overcoming greed, cleansing emotions, beauty, morality.

Blue: Elemental water, love, sensuality, tenderness, emotional healing, artistic endeavors, health and healing, serenity, calm, inner truth, reconstructing, spirit/physical body connection, the power of heaven and the sea, flowing, grace, magickal transformation, femininity, counsel and guidance, meditation, dreaming.

Purple: Loyalty, guidance, clarity, third eye, healing physical pain, spiritual self, mercy, forgiveness, the cauldron, magickal awareness, sleep, balance, harmony, deeper knowledge, aging, divination, prophecy, inspiration, intuition, faith, meditation.

Black: Banishing negativity, aging, death, transformation, change, ghosts, spirits, clairvoyance, prophecy, oracles, divination, storms, vengeance, revenge, protection, deep meditation, overcoming fear, the cauldron, patience, peace, willpower, and life, death, and rebirth.

Brown: Animals, plant life, hearth and home, herbs, grounding, centering, building, construction, conservation of energy, protection, manifestation, comfort, finding that which is lost, recovery, healing animals.

Gray: Balance, justice, harmony, peace, storms, legal matters, banishing confinement, canceling situations, weather, focus, stillness.

White: Purity, elemental spirit, heaven, harmony, compassion, truth, balance, virginity, spiritual helpers, aura healing, overcoming fear, integrating the Higher Self, balancing the bodies, clairvoyance, the All and the Nothing, healing.

Silver: Spirituality, the moon, Goddess energy, abundance, prosperity, dreaming, prophecy, heaven, favorable justice, peace, persistence, water, purging, detoxification, reincarnation, cycles, intuition, aging, ebb and flow, empowerment.

Gold: The sun, energy, abundance, prosperity, the God, masculinity, energy boost, aggressive health and healing, the Infinite, balance of male and female energy, heat, authority, luxury, winning, happiness, success, bridging gaps between self and the Divine, material blessings, brilliance, inspiration.

Rainbow: Happiness, balance, harmony, cycles, reincarnation, nature, birth-death-rebirth, perfect trust.

RED

Aglaia

Aine

Akhushtal

Akwaba

Al-Uzza

Anahit

Anath

Andraste

Apakura

Aphrodite

Asherah

Astarte

Atargatis

Atthar

Auchimalgen

Aurora

Ausrine

Baba Yaga

Baduhenna

Banka-Mundi

Bast Baubo

Bendis

Bia

Biliku

Bona Dea

Brigid

Carna

Chantico

Chicomecoatl

Chuang Mu

Coatlicue

Cocomama

Coyolxauhqui

Cybele

Druantia

Durga

Dzydzilelya

Enekpe

Ereshkigal

The Erinyes

Erzulie

Freya

Frigga

Gunnlod

Haumea

Hel

Hera

Holda

Hsi Wang Mu

Idunn

Inanna

Inari

Indrani

Ishtar

Isis

Ista Devata

Itzpapalotl

Ixtab

Kali Ma

Kamui Fuchi

Kipu-Tytto

Krtya

Kupala

Lakshmi

Lilith

Lofn

Lupa

Macha

Mahuika

Malinalxochitl

Mami Wata

Matsu

Maya

Mayahuel

Medb

Morrigu

Mujaji

Neith

Ninkasi

Nirriti

Odudua

Oenothea

Oshun

Oya

Parvati

Pasiphae

Pele

Persephone

Proserpina

Psyche

Pukkeenegak

Purandhi

Radha

Rangda

Rati

Red Tara

Rhea

Scathach

Sedna

Sekhmet

Sengdroma

Sgeg Mo Ma

Shamhat

Sheela Na Gig

Sita

Sjöfn

Snake Woman

Tap Tun

Tashmetum

Tawaret

Teteoinnan

Tiamat

Tlalteuctli

Tlazolteotl

Tsovinar

Uni

Ushas

Var

Vasudhara
Vellamo
Venus
Yaoji
Yaya Zakurai
The Zorya

ORANGE

Aha Njoku
Akewa
Akonadi
Al-Lat
Anapel
Anath
Arinna
Asase Yaa
Atthar
Aurora
Baba Yaga
Bast
Beiwe
Brogla
Calliope
Ceres
Chasca
Chuang Mu
Cocomama
Dana
Demeter

Durga
Dziewanna
Erzulie
Hestia
Hi'iaka
Idunn
Indrani
Ishtar
Kamui Fuchi
Kuan Yin
Lady Of Beasts
Madre Vieja
Mahuika
Mama Oello
Mawu
Ninkasi
Nuneh
Oshun
Pani
Pax
Persephone
Pomona
Proserpina
Purandhi
Rati
Sekhmet
Shamhat
Shasti
Sita
Tap Tun

Thalia

Tsovinar

Tyche

Ushas

Uzume

Vesna

Vesta

Wakahirume

Yemaya

Zaria

The Zorya

Yellow

Akewa

Alemona

Amaterasu Omikami

Anapel

Apakura

Aphrodite

Arinna

Artemis

Aspelenie

Astghik

Athene

Atthar

Baubo

Beiwe

The Bereginy

Biliku

Bixia Yuanjin

Blodeuwedd

Brigid

Calliope

Carmenta

Ch'ang O

Chasca

Corn Mother

Coyolxauhqui

Creddylad

Cybele

Dewi Nawang Sasih

Diana

Durga

Dziewanna

Elli

Epona

Erzulie

Euphrosyne

Flora

Haumea

Hi'iaka

Idunn

Ilmatar

Indrani

Ishtar

Kuan Yin

Leto

Lucina

Madre Vieja

Maia

Mama Oello

Marama

Matronae

Medb

Metis

Minerva

Minona

Mujaji

Ningal

Nuneh

Onatha

Oshun

Pachamama

Pajau Yan

Parvati

Pax

Pereplut

Persephone

Pomona

Proserpina

Saga

Sarasvati

Saule

Selene

Seshat

Shamhat

Shekinah

Sif

Sól

Tefnut

Thalia

Uni

Ushas

Uttu

Uzume

Vac

The Valkyries

Venus

Vesna

Wakahirume

Xi Hou

Yellow Tara

Yum Chenmo

Zaramama

Zaria

The Zorya

GREEN

Abundantia

Aglaia

Aine

Airmed

Aja

Aje

Al-Lat

Al-Uzza

Anahit

Anuket

Ardwinna

Armathr

Arnamentia

Artemis

Artio

Aryong Jong

Asase Yaa

Ashnan

Astghik

Atargatis

Atira

Axomama

Aziri

Bachué

Banba

Bast

Beiwe

Bendis

The Beregiriy

Blodeuwedd

Boann

Branwen

Brigantia

Brigid

Brogla

Caipora

Carna

Ceres

Chalchiuhtlicue

Chomo-Lung-Ma

Coatlicue

Copia

Corn Mother

Coventina

Creddylad

Cybele

Dana

Demeter

Dewi Nawang Sasih

Don

Druantia

Dugnai

Dziewanna

Eir

Eka Abassi

Eostre

Erce

Ériu

Ertha

Etugen

Feronia

Flidais

Flora

Fódla

Fortuna

Freya

Gaia

Green Tara

Gula

Gunnlod

Gyhldeptis

Habondia

Haltia

Haumea

Hera

Hi'iaka

Idunn

Isis

Jord

Juno

Kamrusepas

Koliada

Kuan Yin

Kupala

Lada

Lakshmi

Leshachikha

Ma Ku

Madre Vieja

Maia

Mama Allpa

Mara

Matronae

Mawu

Mayahuel

Mielikki

Minona

Mokosh

Nana Buluku

Nantosuelta

Nehallenia

Neith

Nekhebet

Nerthus

Ninhursag

Ninti

The Norns

Onatha

Ops

Pachamama

Pani

Papatuanuku

Parvati

Pax

Pinga

Pomona

Purandhi

Renenet

Rhea

Samovila

Sangiyan Sari

Sif

Sigyn

Spider Woman

Tabiti

Thalia

Tyche

Uni

Vasudhara

Ved'Ma

Vesna

Vila

Wadjet

Yama No Kami

Yaoji

Yellow Tara

Zaramama

BLUE

Agemem

Airmed

Akhushtal

Akonadi

Alemona

Al-Lat

Angerona

Antevorta

Anuket

Apakura

Aphrodite

Arachne

Arianrhod

Arnamentia

Aryong Jong

Astarte

Astghik

Atargatis

Ba Ngu'

Bachué

Baduhenna

Banba

Benten

Biliku

Bixia Yuanjin

Blue Tara

Boann

Bona Dea

Brigid

Britomartis

Cailleach

Calliope

Carmenta

Cerridwen

Chalchiuhtlicue

Ch'ang O

Chicomecoatl

Circe

Coatlicue

Copia

Coventina

Dana

Danu

Dike

Don

Eir

Eostre

Ereshkigal

Ériu

Erua

Euphrosyne	Marica
Eurynome	Matsu
Faumea	Meng-Po Niang Niang
Gleti	Mielikki
Gula	Minerva
Gyhldeptis	Mokosh
Hebat	Morrigu
Hel	Mujaji
Hepat	Mulhalmoni
Hera	Nammu
Hine	Nanshe
Ilmatar	Ngame
Ishtar	Ninlil
Ix Chel	Ninsun
Izanami	Nu Kua
Juno	Nut
Kali	Oba
Kamrusepas	Papatuanuku
Kuan Yin	Pax
Lady Of Beasts	Pereplut
Lama	Po Ino Nogar
Lamia	Radha
Leto	Rán
Lofn	Rhea
Lupa	Saga
Ma'at	Samovila
Mama Cocha	Saranyu
Mamlambo	Sarasvati
Manat	Sedna
Marama	Selene

Seshat

Shitala

Sigyn

Sita

Sjöfn

Sophia

Sulis

Sura

Tefnut

Teteoinnan

Thalassa

Tiamat

Tozi

Tsovinar

Uzume

Vac

The Valkyries

Vammatar

Ved'Ma

Vellamo

Venus

Vesna

Xochiquetzal

Yemaya

Zywie

PURPLE

Acpaxapo

Agemem

Aine

Airmed

Aja

The Akkan

Akonadi

Alemona

Ananke

Anath

Angerona

Antevorta

Arianrhod

Banba

Bast

Bellona

The Bereginy

Blodeuwedd

Brigantia

Brigid

Brogla

Cailleach

Caipora

Cerridwen

Chun T'i

Circe

Coventina

Creddylad

Dziewanna

Evaki

Flidais

Gbadu

Gleti

Hathor

Hebat

Hecate

Hera

Inanna

Isis

Kamrusepas

Kamui Fuchi

Kikimora

Krtya

Kupala

Lada

Lajja Gauri

Lama

Lamia

Lilith

Lofn

Ma Ku

Macha

Malinalxochitl

Manat

Marica

Mawu

Mayahuel

Mboze

Medb

Medusa

Meng-Po Niang Niang

Morrigu

Mulhalmoni

Nammu

Nana Buluku

Nanshe

Nephthys

Ngame

Ningal

Ninsun

The Norns

Nut

Oba

Oya

Scathach

Selene

Sheela Na Gig

Siduri Sabitu

Sif

Snake Woman

Sura

Tashmetum

Tuonetar

Ushas

Var

Ved'Ma

Venus

Vesna

Yemaya

Yondung Halmoni

Zaria

BLACK

Acpaxapo

Akhushtal

Ala

Ananke

Andraste

Anna Perenna

Antevorta

Apate

Atira

Ba Ngu'

Badb

Bendis

Black Tara

Cailleach

Cerridwen

Chihucoatl

Circe

Coatlicue

Coventina

Dana

Dike

Don

Eir

Erce

Ereshkigal

The Erinyes

Etugen

Evaki

Freya

Gleti

Hecate

Hel

Hine

Inkosazana

Itzpapalotl

Ixtab

Izanami

Kali

Kikimora

Kipu-Tytto

Krtya

Lamia

Lilith

Lofn

Macha

Mahuika

Mama Allpa

Manat

Manea

The Mar'rallang

Marica

Mati-Syra-Zemlya

Matsu

Maya

Mboze

Medusa

Meskhenet

Morrigu

Musso Koroni

Nanshe

Neith

Nemesis

Nephthys

Ninlil

Nirriti

The Norns

Nut

Odudua

Onatha

Pasiphae

Pele

Pereplut

Persephone

Pinga

Proserpina

Rán

Rangda

Rhiannon

Satine

Scathach

Sekhmet

Sengdroma

Shasti

Sheela Na Gig

Shitala

Spider Woman

Sura

Tabiti

Tashmetum

Tawaret

Teteoinnan

Tiamat

Tlazolteotl

Tozi

Tuonetar

The Valkyries

Vammatar

Yuki Onne

The Zorya

Zywie

Brown

Abundantia

Agemem

Aha Njoku

Airmed

Akwaba

Ardwinna

Artemis

Artio

Asase Yaa

Asherah

Aspelenie

Atira

Axomama

Baba Yaga

Banka-Mundi

Baubo

Bendis

The Bereginy

Britomartis

Brogla

Bugady Musun

Caipora

Carna

Ceres

Chantico

Chomo-Lung-Ma

Cocomama

Corn Mother

Demeter

Diana

Dugnai

Dziewanna

Eka Abassi

Elli

Enekpe

Epona

Erce

Ertha

Etugen

Flidais

Fódla

Gaia

Gbadu

Gula

Gunnlod

Haltia

Hestia

Itzpapalotl

Kamui Fuchi

Kikimora

Kunapipi

Lady Of Beasts

Lama

Leshachikha

Mama Allpa

Mama Oello

Mati-Syra-Zemlya

Matronae

Mawu

Mboze

Meskhenet

Minona

Nana Buluku

Nehallenia

Neith

Nerthus

Ninhursag

The Norns

Nuneh

Oenothea

Ops

Pachamama

Papatuanuku

Pinga

Pukkeenegak

Renenet

Rhiannon

Samovila

Sangiyan Sari

Saranyu

Satine

Sengdroma

Snake Woman

Spider Woman

Tabiti

Tashmetum

Tefnut

Tiamat

Tlalteuctli

Tlazolteotl

Uttu

Vesta

Vila

Yama No Kami

Yaoji

GRAY

Acpaxapo

The Akkan

Ala

Apate

Arianrhod

Armathr

Aryong Jong

Astraea

Athene

Baba Yaga

Baduhenna

Bia

Biliku

Bunzi

Cerridwen

Coatlicue

Dike

Ereshkigal

The Erinyes

Fortuna

Frigga

Gunnlod

Hecate

Hel

Ixtab

Lajja Gauri

Lamia

Lupa

Ma'at

Macha

Manea

Medusa

Musso Koroni

Nemesis

Ngame

The Norns

Po Ino Nogar

Satine

Sheela Na Gig

Shitala

Skadi

Spider Woman

Themis

Tsovinar

Vammatar

Ved'Ma

Yondung Halmoni

WHITE

Aglaia

Aida Wedo

Aja

Akewa

Akhushtal

Ala

Anapel

Anath

Angerona

Aphrodite

Arianrhod

Arinna

Arnamentia

Artemis

Aryong Jong

Asherah

Astarte

Astghik

Astraea

Atargatis

Atthar

Auchimalgen

Ausrine

Beiwe

Bendis

Benten

Bixia Yuanjin

Blodeuwedd

Blue Tara

Boann

Bona Dea

Branwen

Brigid

Brogla

Candelifera

Carmenta

Cerridwen

Ch'ang O

Chihucoatl

Chomo-Lung-Ma

Chun T'i

Chup Kamui

Creddylad

Danu

Dewi Nawang Sasih

Diana

Dike

Dziewanna

Dzydzilelya

Eostre

Ertha

Erzulie

Eurynome

Evaki

Faumea

Feronia

Hecate

Hine

Holda

Hsi Wang Mu

Ilmatar

Inanna

Inari

Inkosazana

Ixtab

Izanami

Koliada

Krtya

Kuan Yin

Lada

Lakshmi

Leto

Lucina

Ma'at

Maia

Mama Cocha

Mami Wata

Manea

The Mar'rallang

Marzanna

Maya

Medusa

Meskhenet

Mokosh

Mulhalmoni

Musso Koroni

Mut

Nammu

Nanshe

Nehallenia

Neith

Nekhebet

Nemesis

Nike

Ningal

Ninlil

Ninti

Pajau Yan

Pasiphae

Pele

Po Ino Nogar

Psyche

Pukkeenegak

Rán

Rangda

Renenet

Rhea

Rhiannon

Saga

Sangiyan Sari

Saranyu

Sarasvati

Satine

Saule

Selene

Sgeg Mo Ma

Shekinah

Siduri Sabitu

Sigyn

Sita

Skadi

Sophia

Sulis

Tefnut

Teteoinnan

Thalia

Themis

Tozi

Tsovinar

Uni

Ushas

Var

Vellamo

Venus

White Buffalo Calf Woman

White Tara

Xi Hou

Yaoji

Yaya Zakurai

Yemaya

Yondung Halmoni

Yuki Onne

SILVER

Acpaxapo

Aine

The Akkan

Alemona

Anapel

Anna Perenna

Antevorta

Aphrodite

Arachne

Arianrhod

Asherah

Ashnan

Astarte

Astraea

Athene

Auchimalgen

Badb

Bellona

Benten

Black Tara	Juno
Cailleach	Krtya
Candelifera	Lajja Gauri
Carna	Lilith
Cerridwen	Ma'at
Ch'ang O	Macha
Chup Kamui	Mama Quilla
Circe	Manat
Dana	Mara
Danu	Marama
Devi	Marica
Diana	Mawu
Don	Medusa
Dzydzilelya	Metis
Eka Abassi	Minerva
Eostre	Morrigu
Erzulie	Nantosuelta
Eurynome	Ngame
Evaki	Nike
Fortuna	Ninsun
Freya	The Norns
Frigga	Nu Kua
Gbadu	Pajau Yan
Gleti	Pasiphae
Habondia	Psyche
Hathor	Radha
Hecate	Red Tara
Hepat	Sarasvati
Hsi Wang Mu	Selene
Inanna	Sgeg Mo Ma

Shakti

Sheela Na Gig

Siduri Sabitu

Sigyn

Skadi

Thalassa

Themis

Tozi

Uni

Ushas

Vellamo

Vesna

Wakahirume

White Tara

Yaoji

Zaramama

Zaria

The Zorya

GOLD

Abundantia

Aje

Akewa

Akwaba

Amaterasu Omikami

Anuket

Aphrodite

Armathr

Artemis

Artio

Aspelenie

Atthar

Aurora

Ausrine

Aziri

Bast

Black Tara

Brigid

Candelifera

Chasca

Chomo-Lung-Ma

Chuang Mu

Chun T'i

Copia

Coventina

Coyolxauhqui

Devi

Durga

Dzydzilelya

Eostre

Erua

Flora

Fortuna

Freya

Gullveig

Habondia

Hathor

Hepat

Idunn

Inanna

Inari

Ishtar

Isis

Juno

Krtya

Kuan Yin

Lajja Gauri

Lakshmi

Mama Quilla

Mamlambo

Mara

Marzanna

Matronae

Medb

Meskhenet

Metis

Nantosuelta

Nehallenia

Neith

Nekhebet

Nephthys

Nike

Ninkasi

Ninti

Nut

Onatha

Ops

Oshun

Pereplut

Purandhi

Renenet

Rhiannon

Saga

Saule

Sekhmet

Seshat

Shakti

Shamhat

Sif

Sita

Sól

Tabiti

Tawaret

Tefnut

Thalia

Themis

Uni

Uzume

Vac

Vasudhara

Venus

Wadjet

Wakahirume

White Tara

Xi Hou

Xochiquetzal

Yellow Tara

Yum Chenmo
Zaria
The Zorya

Rainbow
Aida Wedo
Amaterasu Omikami
Bunzi
Estsanatlehi
Fravashi

Hina
Inkosazana
Iris
Ix Chel
Julunggul
Kunapipi
Mbaba Mwana Waresa
Nu Kua
Shakti
White Buffalo Calf Woman

FOUR

· · · · · · · · · · ✳ · · · · · · · · · ·

The Elements

The four elements are the basic principles of magickal practice, and the foundation of all that exists. Earth, air, fire, and water are the physical and spiritual components of the universe, and each is a force of energy that contributes to the existence of life.

Each element has a variety of correspondences, as well as emotional and physical manifestations.

Earth: Grounding, prosperity, abundance, material blessings, money, nature, harvest, fertility, growth, silence, calm, harmony, balance, recovering, healing, peace, plants and herbs, home, morality, protection, motherhood, silence, birth, death, mystery, structures, physical body, winter.

Air: Intellect, wisdom, memory, learning, knowledge, study, mental clarity, happiness, joy, cheerfulness, divination, self-knowledge, confidence, vitality, energy, elemental air, springtime, artistic endeavors, magick, travel, speaking, writing.

Fire: Summertime, passion, desire, transformation, sex, anger, protection, punishment, justice, law, banishing, spirits, success, legal matters, prophecy, oracles, independence, transmutation, healing, the arts, inspiration, authority, creating and destroying.

Water: Prophecy, oracles, love, emotions, sleep, dreaming, meditation, friendships, relationships, serenity, peace, calm, advice, counseling, sensuality, divination, intuition, autumn, acceptance, empathy, health and healing.

EARTH

Abundantia

Agemem

Aglaia

Aha Njoku

Airmed

Aja

Aje

Akhushtal

Ala

Al-Lat

Ananke

Andraste

Anna Perenna

Anuket

Ardwinna

Armathr

Artemis

Artio

Asase Yaa

Asherah

Ashnan

Aspelenie

Atargatis

Atira

Axomama

Banba

Banka-Mundi

Beiwe

Bendis

The Bereginy

Black Tara

Bona Dea

Branwen

Brigantia

Britomartis

Brogla

Bugady Musun

Bunzi

Caipora

Carna

Ceres

Chantico

Chicomecoatl

Chomo-Lung-Ma

Chun T'i

Coatlicue

Cocomama

Copia

Corn Mother

Coyolxauhqui

Creddylad

Cybele

Dana

Demeter

Devi

Dewi Nawang Sasih

Diana

Don

Druantia

Dugnai

Durga

Dziewanna

Eka Abassi

Elli

Enekpe

Eostre

Epona

Erce

Ereshkigal

Ériu

Ertha

Erua

Estsanatlehi

Etugen

Eurynome

Feronia

Flidais

Flora

Fódla

Fortuna

Frigga

Gaia

Gula

Gunnlod

Gyhldeptis

Habondia

Haltia

Haumea

Hebat

Hecate

Hel

Hekit

Hestia

Hi'iaka

Hine

Holda

Idunn

Inari

Isis

Itzpapalotl

Jord

Juno

Kali Ma

Kamui Fuchi

Kikimora

Koliada

Krtya

Kunapipi

Lady of Beasts

Leshachikha

Lupa

Ma Ku

Macha

Madre Vieja

Maia

Mama Allpa

Mama Oello

The Mar'rallang

Mara

Mati-Syra-Zemlya

Matronae

Mawu

Mayahuel

Medb

Meskhenet

Mielikki

Minona

Mokosh

Nana Buluku

Nantosuelta

Nehallenia

Nekhebet

Nephthys

Nerthus

Ninhursag

Ninsun

Ninti

The Norns

Nuneh

Odudua

Oenothea

Onatha

Ops

Pachamama

Pani

Papatuanuku

Pax

Persephone

Pinga

Pomona

Proserpina

Pukkeenegak

Purandhi

Renenet

Rhea

Rhiannon

Samovila

Sangiyan Sari

Saranyu

Satine

Sengdroma

Shakti

Shasti

Sheela Na Gig

Shekinah

Sif

Sigyn

Skadi

Snake Woman

Spider Woman

Tabiti

Tashmetum

Tawaret

Teteoinnan

Thalia

Tlalteuctli

Tozi

Tuonetar

Tyche

Uni

Uttu

Var

Vasudhara

Vesna

Vesta

Vila

Wadjet

White Buffalo Calf Woman

Xochiquetzal

Yama No Kami

Yaoji

Yellow Tara

Zaramama

Zywie

AIR

Agemem

Aglaia

Aida Wedo

Akhushtal

Akonadi

Alemona

Al-Lat

Amaterasu Omikami

Ananke

Angerona

Apate

Arianrhod

Arinna

Artemis

Astarte

Astraea

Athene

Aurora

Ausrine

Baba Yaga

Baduhenna

Banba

Bast

Baubo

Bendis

Benten

The Bereginy

Bixia

Blodeuwedd

Blue Tara

Brigantia

Brigid

Brogla

Cailleach

Calliope

Candelifera

Carmenta

Ch'ang O

Chasca

Creddylad

Diana

Dike	Metis
Don	Minerva
Eka Abassi	Musso Koroni
Elli	Mut
Eostre	Ngame
Eurynome	Nike
Faumea	Ningal
Fravashi	Ninlil
Gleti	Ninti
Green Tara	Nu Kua
Hera	Nuneh
Hi'iaka	Nut
Hina	Oya
Holda	Pasiphae
Hsi Wang Mu	Psyche
Ilmatar	Saga
Inkosazana	Saranyu
Isis	Seshat
Izanami	Shakti
Juno	Shekinah
Kali Ma	Sita
Krtya	Skadi
Lajja Gauri	Sophia
Leto	Spider Woman
Lilith	Tefnut
Lucina	Themis
Ma'at	Tlalteuctli
The Mar'rallang	Uni
Maya	Ushas
Mbaba Mwana Waresa	Uzume

Vac

The Valkyries

Var

Vasudhara

Vesna

Wakahirume

White Tara

Xi Hou

Yaya Zakurai

Yellow Tara

Yondung Halmoni

Yuanjin

Yuki Onne

Yum Chenmo

Zaria

FIRE

Acpaxapo

Aglaia

Aida Wedo

Akewa

Akonadi

Al-Lat

Amaterasu Omikami

Anahit

Ananke

Anath

Andraste

Arachne

Arinna

Aspelenie

Astarte

Athene

Atthar

Auchimalgen

Aurora

Ausrine

Baba Yaga

Badb

Baduhenna

Banka-Mundi

Bast

Beiwe

Bellona

Bia

Biliku

Black Tara

Brigantia

Brigid

Candelifera

Carna

Chantico

Chasca

Chihucoatl

Chuang Mu

Chun T'i

Coatlicue

Cybele

Druantia

Durga

Ereshkigal

The Erinyes

Erzulie

Eurynome

Evaki

Feronia

Gullveig

Hera

Inanna

Indrani

Ishtar

Isis

Ista Devata

Ixtab

Kali Ma

Kamrusepas

Kamui Fuchi

Kipu-Tytto

Krtya

Kupala

Lama

Lilith

Lofn

Lupa

Mahuika

Malinalxochitl

Manea

The Mar'rallang

Marzanna

Mayahuel

Medb

Medusa

Morrigu

Nemesis

Ninti

Nirriti

Pele

Radha

Rangda

Rati

Red Tara

Saule

Scathach

Sekhmet

Sengdroma

Shakti

Shasti

Sita

Snake Woman

Sól

Tap Tun

Tawaret

Tefnut

Tlazolteotl

Tsovinar

Ushas

The Valkyries

Vammatar

Vasudhara

Wadjet

Xi Hou

The Zorya

WATER

Acpaxapo

Aida Wedo

Aine

Airmed

Aja

Akhushtal

The Akkan

Akwaba

Alemona

Al-Lat

Al-Uzza

Anahit

Anapel

Anna Perenna

Antevorta

Anuket

Apakura

Aphrodite

Arachne

Arianrhod

Arnamentia

Aryong Jong

Asherah

Astarte

Astghik

Astraea

Atargatis

Auchimalgen

Aziri

Ba Ngu'

Bachué

Badb

Bast

Baubo

Benten

Biliku

Blodeuwedd

Boann

Branwen

Brigantia

Brigid

Britomartis

Bunzi

Cailleach

Calliope

Carmenta

Cerridwen

Chalchiuhtlicue

Ch'ang O

Chuang Mu

Chun T'i

Chup Kamui

Circe

Cocomama

Coventina	Ix Chel
Dana	Izanami
Danu	Julunggul
Don	Kali Ma
Dzydzilelya	Kamrusepas
Eir	Krtya
Erua	Kuan Yin
Erzulie	Kupala
Euphrosyne	Lada
Eurynome	Lakshmi
Evaki	Lamia
Faumea	Leto
Feronia	Lofn
Freya	Mama Cocha
Frigga	Mama Quilla
Gbadu	Mami Wata
Green Tara	Mamlambo
Gula	Manat
Gyhldeptis	Manea
Hathor	Marama
Hekit	Marica
Holda	The Mar'rallang
Ilmatar	Marzanna
Inanna	Matsu
Inkosazana	Maya
Iris	Mbaba Mwana Waresa
Ishtar	Mboze
Isis	Medusa
Itzpapalotl	Meng-Po Niang Niang

Minerva

Mokosh

Morrigu

Mujaji

Mulhalmoni

Nammu

Nanshe

Nantosuelta

Neith

Nephthys

Ngame

Ningal

Ninkasi

Ninlil

Ninsun

Ninti

The Norns

Nu Kua

Nut

Oba

Oenothea

Oshun

Pajau Yan

Papatuanuku

Parvati

Pasiphae

Pereplut

Po Ino Nogar

Psyche

Radha

Rán

Rati

Rhea

Saga

Sarasvati

Saule

Sedna

Selene

Sgeg Mo Ma

Shakti

Shamhat

Sheela Na Gig

Shitala

Siduri Sabitu

Sjöfn

Sulis

Sura

Tefnut

Thalassa

Thalia

Tiamat

Tlalteuctli

Tlazolteotl

Tozi

Tsovinar

Tuonetar

Uzume

The Valkyries

Vasudhara

Ved'Ma

Vellamo

Venus

Wadjet

White Tara

Xochiquetzal

Yaya Zakurai

Yemaya

Zaria

Zywie

· · · · · · · · · · · ❋ · · · · · · · · · · ·

FIVE

The Wheel of the Year

The Wheel of the Year is a Neo-Pagan calendar that tracks the earth's natural cycle of seasons. Within the Wheel are eight Sabbats, or festivals. These festivals embody the birth, life, and death of the earth as it journeys on its infinite and circular path through the cosmos. Within this cycle, the light and the dark will embark on their yearly course where power is shifted and split between them. At its height, the light will spread its vibrant rays and produce life and fulfillment. At it lowest point, the light will give way to the darkness that allows the land rest and dormancy. Though polar opposites, both the light and the dark bring forth the gifts necessary for balance and harmony. Within the eight Sabbats balance is created, allowing us to celebrate the wonders and gifts brought about by each season.

Yule: Winter solstice. The Wheel begins deep within the darkness as the Goddess gives birth to the Horned God. In His infant stage, He represents the planted seed awaiting growth. Although the earth appears dormant, the cycle of life has just been reborn beneath its surface. Yule is a time for potential, growth, expectancy, rest, hope, healing, and new beginnings. This time of darkness enables us to go inside and reflect on our own potential as well as the world's. Through rest and reflection, we can fully envision what gifts we might bring about at the sun's return.

Imbolc: February 2nd. The Horned God begins to grow and strengthen, but is not yet at full power. Meanwhile, as the Goddess is healing from Her birth of the Horned God, She begins to cleanse Herself in preparation of Her return to the Maiden form. As the ice will soon thaw and the earth grow fertile once more, we are reminded of the journey that lies ahead and the preparations needed. Imbolc is a time for purification, dedication, cleansing, initiation, and preparation. While the sun begins to gain strength, we might take the opportunity to wipe away negativity—and open up to the blessings and insight needed to move forward.

Ostara: Spring equinox. At this point on the Wheel, The Horned God enjoys youthful vigor while the Goddess, now a young Maiden, spreads Her fertility across the land. With these events set in motion, the God may begin His courtship with the Goddess. Now that the sun is quickly growing in strength and the soil is fertile, the seed that once lay dormant has finally begun to sprout. Ostara is a time for balance, awakenings, fertility, and vitality. As night and day have found complete balance, we should come to understand the many facets of ourselves in order to create a balance for the long journey ahead.

Beltane: May 1st. The Horned God has now entered into manhood and joins the Maiden in both a sexual and spiritual union. At Her fertile peak, the Maiden now prepares for Her transformation into Mother. Beltane marks the fullest point of spring. The soil is flourishing with fresh growth and all things are full of life. While the sun is nearing its highest potential, we may now take the liberty of celebrating our endeavors with those around us. Beltane is a time for unity, celebration, sexuality, growth, fertility, and love. The true spirit of the season calls us to enjoy every aspect of our beauty and not to be ashamed of the gifts that we bring to the universe.

Litha: Summer solstice. With the Goddess now ripe and pregnant, the Horned God is at His highest point of power. The earth and its inhabitants are now in full bloom and rich with energy. Summer solstice is the counter to Yule on the Wheel now turning to let balance commence. Summer solstice is a time for abundance, ripeness, passion, energy, and empowerment. With the harvest coming soon, we must allow ourselves to celebrate the wonders we have accomplished and trust that the rewards will soon be reaped.

Lammas: August 1st. The Horned God and His light are now beginning to fade. The Goddess does not mourn, for She knows within Her lies His rebirth. As the land is full and ripe, the time for harvesting has begun. Lammas is a time for acceptance, talent, fullness, and improvement. The season brings out the opportunity for us to learn about the great gifts we have received, and how we might use these gifts to better ourselves and others.

Mabon: Autumn equinox. The Horned God is now in preparation for His body to be received into the underworld. In its deepest harvest, the earth gives forth its gifts in great abundance. Although the harvest is plentiful, the rich colors brought forth from summer solstice are now fading as the land is preparing for its slumber. Mabon is a time for thanks, preservation, reflection, preparation, and abundance. At this point of the cycle, we are reminded to give thanks for what we have received, both good and bad, and to concentrate on the future.

Samhain: October 31st. The Horned God passes from one world to the next and patiently awaits His rebirth. The Goddess, as a Crone, again prepares for Her birth of the Horned God. At the year's last harvest, we are called to take account of all things received in our lives. Samhain is a time for deep reflection, inventory, blessings, letting go, and trust. While the cycle nears completion, we must find the will to release the things in our lives that no longer hold bearings. In this release, through celebration, we will hope to reach divination.

YULE

Akhushtal

The Akkan

Akwaba

Ala

Alemona

Al-Uzza

Anapel

Angerona

Antevorta

Apakura

Arianrhod

Armathr

Arnamentia

Aspelenie

Bixia Yuanjin

Boann

Bona Dea

Cailleach

Candelifera

Carmenta

Carna

Cerridwen

Chalchiuhtlicue

Coatlicue

Coventina

Dana

Demeter

Don

Druantia

Eka Abassi

Erce

Erua

Eurynome

Evaki

Freya

Frigga

Gleti

Gula

Hebat

Hecate

Hekit

Hel

Hera

Holda

Idunn

Isis

Izanami

Kali Ma

Koliada

Lamia

Leto

Lucina

Lupa

Mama Oello

Manat

Marzanna

Mayahuel

Meskhenet

Nana Buluku

Nekhebet

Ningal

Ninhursag

Ninlil

Ninsun

Ninti

The Norns

Nuneh

Oenothea

Pasiphae

Pukkeenegak

Rán

Renenet

Rhea

Rhiannon

Saga

Saule

Sedna

Selene

Seshat

Shasti

Shekinah

Sigyn

Skadi

Sól

Sophia

Sulis

Tawaret

Tefnut

Tiamat

Tozi

Ushas

The Valkyries

Var

Ved'Ma

Wadjet

Xi Hou

Yaya Zakurai

Yuki Onne

Yum Chenmo

The Zorya

Zywie

Imbolc

Akwaba

Alemona

Al-Uzza

Anapel

Antevorta

Arnamentia

Astarte

Astraea

Auchimalgen

Ba Ngu'

Banba

Baubo

Blue Tara

Boann

Brigid

Cailleach

Candelifera

Carmenta

Ch'ang O

Chomo-Lung-Ma

Chup Kamui

Coventina

Dana

Danu

Devi

Diana

Dike

Don

Epona

Erce

Ériu

Green Tara

Gullveig

Hecate

Hestia

Hina

Ista Devata

Julunggul

Kamrusepas

Kuan Yin

Kunapipi

Lajja Gauri

Lama

Mama Cocha

The Mar'rallang

Matsu

Meskhenet

Minerva

Ninsun

Nu Kua

Oya

Pachamama

Pajau Yan

Pele

Pereplut

Pinga

Psyche

Rhiannon

Saranyu

Saule

Scathach

Sekhmet

Selene

Sgeg Mo Ma

Shakti

Shekinah

Sigyn

Sjöfn

Skadi

Snake Woman

Sól

Sulis

Teteoinnan

Thalassa

Tlalteuctli

Tozi

Tsovinar

Ushas

Uttu

Vammatar

Var

Vesna

Vesta

Wadjet

Wakahirume

Xi Hou

Yemaya

Yum Chenmo

The Zorya

Ostara

Aglaia

The Akkan

Alemona

Al-Uzza

Anath

Andraste

Anna Perenna

Aphrodite

Arachne

Artemis

Asase Yaa

Asherah

Ashnan

Aspelenie

Astarte

Atargatis

Aurora

Ausrine

Aziri

Bast

Beiwe

The Bereginy

Bia

Bixia Yuanjin

Blodeuwedd

Branwen

Britomartis

Bunzi

Cailleach

Calliope

Carmenta

Carna

Chun T'i

Corn Mother

Creddylad

Cybele

Demeter

Dewi Nawang Sasih

Dike

Dziewanna

Dzydzilelya

Eostre

Erce

Ertha

Estsanatlehi

Euphrosyne

Eurynome

Flidais

Flora

Gaia

Gbadu

Green Tara

Gyhldeptis

Hathor

Hebat

Hekit

Hi'iaka

Hsi Wang Mu

Idunn

Ilmatar

Inkosazana

Iris

Ishtar

Isis

Ix Chel

Juno

Kikimora

Kuan Yin

Lada

Lajja Gauri

Lakshmi

Leshachikha

Lupa

Ma Ku

Ma'at

Madre Vieja

Maia

Mama Allpa

Mama Oello

The Mar'rallang

Marama

Marzanna

Matronae

Mawu

Mayahuel

Mujaji

Mut

Nantosuelta

Nehallenia

Nekhebet

Nerthus

Ngame

Ninhursag

Onatha

Ops

Pajau Yan

Parvati

Pasiphae

Pax

Persephone

Po Ino Nogar

Pomona

Proserpina
Purandhi
Renenet
Rhea
Sangiyan Sari
Sarasvati
Seshat
Sgeg Mo Ma
Shakti
Shasti
Shekinah
Sigyn
Sjöfn
Tabiti
Thalia
Themis
Tlalteuctli
Tozi
Tyche
Uttu
Uzume
Vellamo
Venus
Vesna
Wadjet
Xochiquetzal
Yaoji
Yaya Zakurai
Zaramama
Zaria

BELTANE

Agemem
Aine
Akwaba
Al-Uzza
Anath
Aphrodite
Armathr
Asherah
Astarte
Ausrine
Bast
Beiwe
Bendis
Benten
Blodeuwedd
Bona Dea
Branwen
Brigantia
Caipora
Calliope
Chuang Mu
Cocomama
Creddylad
Cybele
Devi
Dzydzilelya
Eostre
Erce

Ereshkigal	Nike
Erua	Ningal
Etugen	Ninlil
Euphrosyne	Nut
Faumea	Oba
Flidais	Parvati
Flora	Persephone
Freya	Proserpina
Frigga	Psyche
Gunnlod	Radha
Hathor	Rati
Haumea	Red Tara
Hera	Sarasvati
Hi'iaka	Shekinah
Hina	Sita
Inanna	Sjöfn
Indrani	Sophia
Jord	Sura
Lada	Tap Tun
Lakshmi	Tashmetum
Lofn	Uni
Lupa	Uzume
Mama Quilla	Var
Mawu	Venus
Mbaba Mwana Waresa	Vesna
Mielikki	Vila
Minerva	Xochiquetzal
Mujaji	Yaya Zakurai

LITHA

Aine

Aje

Akewa

Akhushtal

Akonadi

Al-Uzza

Amaterasu Omikami

Anahit

Anath

Aphrodite

Arinna

Asherah

Astarte

Astghik

Atargatis

Atthar

Aurora

Bast

Baubo

Bellona

Bendis

Benten

Bia

Brigantia

Brogla

Ch'ang O

Chantico

Chasca

Chuang Mu

Circe

Cocomama

Copia

Cybele

Devi

Diana

Druantia

Dzydzilelya

Elli

Erce

Ertha

Erzulie

Eurynome

Evaki

Flidais

Fortuna

Freya

Hathor

Inanna

Indrani

Ishtar

Isis

Ista Devata

Itzpapalotl

Ix Chel

Ixtab

Juno

Kali Ma

Kupala

Lady of Beasts

Lilith

Lofn

Mama Quilla

Mami Wata

Mara

Marica

Maya

Mboze

Medb

Metis

Morrigu

Mut

Nammu

Nike

Ningal

Odudua

Parvati

Pasiphae

Pele

Persephone

Proserpina

Psyche

Purandhi

Radha

Rati

Red Tara

Renenet

Saga

Samovila

Sarasvati

Saule

Scathach

Sekhmet

Sengdroma

Seshat

Shakti

Shamhat

Sheela Na Gig

Sif

Sita

Sjöfn

Snake Woman

Sól

Tap Tun

Tefnut

Tlalteuctli

Tlazolteotl

Tozi

Tsovinar

Uni

Ushas

Uzume

Vac

The Valkyries

Venus

Vila

Wadjet

Xi Hou

Xochiquetzal

Yaoji

Yemaya

Zaria

LAMMAS

Abundantia

Aha Njoku

Airmed

Aja

Aje

Akonadi

Al-Lat

Al-Uzza

Anuket

Ardwinna

Artio

Aryong Jong

Asase Yaa

Ashnan

Atargatis

Athene

Atira

Axomama

Aziri

The Bereginy

Brigantia

Bunzi

Ceres

Chalchiuhtlicue

Ch'ang O

Chomo-Lung-Ma

Copia

Corn Mother

Coventina

Dana

Danu

Demeter

Diana

Dugnai

Durga

Dziewanna

Elli

Enekpe

Epona

Erce

Ertha

Estsanatlehi

Feronia

Flora

Fódla

Fortuna

Gaia

Gula

Habondia

Haltia

Haumea

Hestia

Inari

Jord

Juno

Kamrusepas

Kamui Fuchi

Kikimora

Lajja Gauri

Lakshmi

Leto

Mama Allpa

Mamlambo

Mara

Mati-Syra-Zemlya

Mbaba Mwana Waresa

Medb

Mielikki

Minona

Mokosh

Nana Buluku

Nantosuelta

Nehallenia

Nerthus

Ngame

Ninkasi

Ninti

Nuneh

Oba

Oenothea

Ops

Pachamama

Pani

Papatuanuku

Pereplut

Po Ino Nogar

Pukkeenegak

Rhea

Shitala

Sif

Sigyn

Spider Woman

Teteoinnan

Tozi

Uni

Vasudhara

Vesta

White Buffalo Calf Woman

White Tara

Yama No Kami

Yaoji

Yellow Tara

Zaramama

MABON

Abundantia

Aha Njoku

Aja

Al-Lat

Al-Uzza

Anuket

Apakura

Arachne

Artio

Aryong Jong

Asase Yaa

Ashnan

Athene

Atira

Axomama

Banka-Mundi

Biliku

Blue Tara

Bugady Musun

Bunzi

Caipora

Ceres

Chalchiuhtlicue

Chantico

Chicomecoatl

Copia

Corn Mother

Coyolxauhqui

Dana

Demeter

Dewi Nawang Sasih

Diana

Dike

Don

Dugnai

Eir

Enekpe

Erce

Feronia

Fódla

Gbadu

Gullveig

Gyhldeptis

Hestia

Inari

Isis

Jord

Kali Ma

Kamui Fuchi

Kikimora

Kipu-Tytto

Kuan Yin

Lady of Beasts

Ma'at

Madre Vieja

Malinalxochitl

Mama Allpa

Mama Cocha

Mamlambo

The Mar'rallang

Marama

Mati-Syra-Zemlya

Matronae

Mawu

Mboze

Medb

Minona

Nemesis

Nike

Ninhursag

Ninkasi

Nirriti

Onatha

Ops

Pachamama

Pani

Pasiphae

Pinga

Po Ino Nogar

Pomona

Pukkeenegak

Renenet

Samovila

Sangiyan Sari

Saranyu

Scathach

Sedna

Sengdroma

Shakti

Sif

Snake Woman

Spider Woman

Tabiti

Tefnut

Teteoinnan

Themis

Tlalteuctli

Vac

Vesta

Vila

White Buffalo Calf Woman

White Tara

Yama No Kami

Yaoji

Yellow Tara

Yemaya

Yondung Halmoni

Zaramama

SAMHAIN

Acpaxapo

Agemem

Aida Wedo

Airmed

The Akkan

Akonadi

Ala

Al-Uzza

Ananke

Anapel

Anath

Andraste

Antevorta

Apate

Arianrhod

Arnamentia

Athene

Auchimalgen

Ba Ngu'

Baba Yaga

Bachué

Badb

Baduhenna

Banka-Mundi

Bendis

Biliku

Black Tara

Blue Tara

Cailleach

Cerridwen

Chalchiuhtlicue

Chihucoatl

Chun T'i

Circe

Coatlicue

Coyolxauhqui

Diana

Durga

Eir

Eka Abassi

Elli

Enekpe

Erce

Ereshkigal

The Erinyes

Erzulie

Eurynome

Evaki

Fravashi

Gbadu

Gleti

Gula

Gullveig

Gunnlod

Hecate

Hel

Hera

Hine

Hsi Wang Mu

Inanna

Indrani

Ishtar

Isis

Itzpapalotl

Ix Chel

Ixtab

Izanami

Julunggul

Kali Ma

Kikimora

Kipu-Tytto

Krtya

Kunapipi

Lajja Gauri

Lama

Lamia

Leshachikha

Lilith

Ma Ku

Macha

Mahuika

Malinalxochitl

Manat

Manea

Marama

Marica

Maya

Medusa

Meng-Po Niang Niang

Meskhenet

Metis

Morrigu

Mulhalmoni

Musso Koroni

Mut

Nammu

Nana Buluku

Nanshe

Neith

Nemesis

Nephthys

Ningal

Ninlil

Ninsun

Nirriti

The Norns

Nu Kua

Nut

Onatha

Oya

Pajau Yan

Pasiphae

Pele

Persephone

Pinga

Proserpina

Rán

Rangda

Red Tara

Satine

Scathach

Sekhmet

Shamhat

Sheela Na Gig

Shitala

Siduri Sabitu

Skadi

Snake Woman

Sophia

Sura

Tashmetum

Tawaret

Tiamat

Tlazolteotl

Tuonetar

Ushas

The Valkyries

Vammatar

Ved'Ma

Yemaya

Yondung Halmoni

Yuki Onne

The Zorya

Zywie

SIX

························ ✳ ·······················

Maiden, Mother, Crone

In his book *The White Goddess,* Robert Graves categorizes the Divine Feminine into three aspects: Maiden, Mother, and Crone. These three aspects, now known as The Triple Goddess, classify Her many faces, aligning Her phases and power with the stages of a woman's life.

These three aspects can be defined further, into shadow and light characterizations.

The Light Maiden is the first aspect of the Triple Goddess. In human terms, her age is birth to early twenties. She is the little girl blossoming into womanhood, the image of beauty and love. She is the discovery of femininity. The embodiment of youth, learning, playfulness, and new beginnings, the Maiden is the personification of spring.

The Dark Maiden is the shadow side of the Light Maiden. She is the seductress, the energy of passion and lust, the dark, mysterious side of youth. She is the Manipulator, taking Her new knowledge of life and love and using it to Her advantage. At times, She is the Betrayer, the Oracle, or the Psychopomp—embracing the darkness of existence and speaking Her truth, regardless of the consequences.

The Mother aspect of the Goddess is at the peak of power and life. She is in control of Her circumstances and Her sexuality, and is usually mated. She is the harvest, the representation of abundance and prosperity, and our true Earth Mother. She is the midwife and protector of children, whether or not they are Hers. The Mother is strength, resilience, and the knowledge of womanhood.

The Dark Mother is the personification of anger, transformation, wars on the physical plane, and battles within spiritual mindfields. She is the blackness of the new moon: the active, pulsing aggression that moves cycles forward and erases fear from our consciousness. She is the harbinger of death and change, justice and vengeance, forcing us to sacrifice that which no longer serves.

The Light Crone is the Wise Woman, She of the Kept Blood (menopause). She is the guide, the counselor, and the infinite teacher. She brings us to death in all its terrible fury, then holds and nurtures us as we are reborn. She is the darkness of winter, and teaches the power of intuition and how to see what is unseen.

The Dark Crone is the Hag, the Keeper of Time and the Infinite. She is the All and the Nothing, the chaotic order of the universe and all that it embraces.

LIGHT MAIDENS

Abundantia

Aglaia

Aje

Al-Uzza

Anath

Angerona

Anna Perenna

Aphrodite

Arachne

Ardwinna

Artemis

Ashnan

Astghik

Atargatis

Athene

Aurora

Ausrine

Bast

Baubo

Beiwe

Benten

The Bereginy

Boann

Branwen

Brigid

Britomartis

Bunzi

Calliope

Carna

Ch'ang O

Chasca

Chuang Mu

Chup Kamui

Corn Woman

Creddylad

Diana

Dike

Dziewanna

Dzydzilelya

Eostre

Erzulie

Estsanatlehi

Euphrosyne

Flidais

Flora

Freya

Gbadu

Green Tara

Gullveig

Hathor

Haumea

Hestia

Hi'iaka

Idunn

Ilmatar

Inanna

Inkosazana

Iris

Ista Devata

Lada

Lama

The Mar'rallang

Matsu Maya

Mbaba Mwana Waresa

Mielikki

Minerva

Minona

Nehallenia

Ngame

Nike

Ningal

Ninlil

Onatha

Oshun

Pajau Yan

Parvati

Pax

Persephone

Pinga

Pomona

Proserpina

Psyche

Purandhi

Radha

Sarasvati

Sedna

Selene

Sgeg Mo Ma

Sif

Sigyn

Sita

Sjöfn

Sulis

Sura

Tefnut

Thalia

Tsovinar

Tyche

Ushas

Uttu

Uzume

Vellamo

Venus

Vesna

Vesta

Vila

Wakahirume

Xochiquetzal

Yaoji

Yaya Zakurai

Zaria

The Zorya

Dark Maidens

Aine

Al-Uzza

Anath

Apate

Aphrodite

Arachne

Artemis

Astarte

Astraea

Athene

Bendis

Blodeuwedd

Chicomecoatl

Circe

Coyolxauhqui

Dzydzilelya

Eir

Erzulie

Freya

Freya

Gunnlod

Inanna

Indrani

Ishtar

Ixtab

Kipu-Tytto

Lilith

Lofn

Mami Wata

The Mar'rallang

Marama

Marica

Musso Koroni

Nemesis

Nephthys

Ngame

Ningal

Ninlil

Onatha

Oshun

Persephone

Proserpina

Rati

Shamhat

Sif

Snake Woman

Tap Tun

Tlazolteotl

Tuonetar

The Valkyries

Vammatar

Venus

Vila

Yuki Onne

LIGHT MOTHERS

Agemem

Aha Njoku

Aida Wedo

Airmed

Aje

The Akkan

Akewa

Akhushtal

Akwaba

Ala

Alemona

Al-Lat

Amaterasu Omikami

Anahit

Andraste

Anuket

Arianrhod

Arinna

Armathr

Arnamentia

Artio

Aryong Jong

Asase Yaa

Asherah

Aspelenie

Astarte

Atira

Atthar

Auchimalgen

Axomama

Aziri

Ba Ngu'

Bachué

Banba

Bixia Yuanjin

Blue Tara

Bona Dea

Brigantia

Brigid

Brogla

Caipora

Candelifera

Carmenta

Ceres

Chalchiuhtlicue

Chicomecoatl

Chomo-Lung-Ma

Chun T'i

Cocomama

Copia

Corn Woman

Coventina

Dana

Danu

Demeter

Devi

Dewi Nawang Sasih

Diana

Don

Druantia

Dugnai

Eka Abassi

Enekpe

Epona

Erce

Ériu

Ertha

Erua

Estsanatlehi

Etugen

Eurynome

Faumea

Feronia

Fódla

Fortuna

Fravashi

Frigga

Gaia

Gleti

Green Tara

Gula

Gyhldeptis

Habondia

Haltia

Haumea

Hebat

Hekit

Hera

Hina

Hsi Wang Mu

Ilmatar

Inari

Ishtar

Ix Chel

Izanami

Jord

Julunggul

Juno

Kamrusepas

Kamui Fuchi

Kikimora

Kuan Yin

Kupala

Lady of Beasts

Lajja Gauri

Lakshmi

Leshachikha

Leto

Lucina

Ma Ku

Ma'at

Maia

Mama Allpa

Mama Cocha

Mama Oello

Mama Quilla

Mamlambo

Mati-Syra-Zemlya

Matronae

Mawu

Mayahuel

Mboze

Meskhenet

Mujaji

Mut

Nammu

Nantosuelta

Nekhebet

Nerthus

Ngame

Ninkasi

Ninsun

Ninti

Nu Kua

Nuneh

Nut

Oba

Odudua

Oenothea

Ops

Pachamama

Pani

Papatuanuku

Pasiphae

Pereplut

Po Ino Nogar

Pukkeenegak

Renenet

Rhea

Rhiannon

Sangiyan Sari

Saranyu

Saule

Sengdroma

Seshat

Shakti

Shasti

Shekinah

Siduri Sabitu

Snake Woman

Sól

Sophia

Tabiti

Tashmetum

Tawaret

Teteoinnan

Thalassa

Themis

Uni

Vac

Var

Vasudhara

Wadjet

White Buffalo Calf Woman

White Tara

Xi Hou

Yama No Kami

Yellow Tara

Yemaya

Yum Chenmo

Zaramama

The Zorya

DARK MOTHERS

Andraste
Apakura
Asase Yaa
Auchimalgen
Badb
Baduhenna
Banka-Mundi
Bellona
Bia
Biliku
Black Tara
Blue Tara
Ceres
Chalchiuhtlicue
Chantico
Chicomecoatl
Chihucoatl
Coatlicue
Cybele
Durga
Hera
Hine
Holda
Hsi Wang Mu
Itzpapalotl
Juno
Lamia
Lupa

Mahuika
Malinalxochitl
Medb
Morrigu
Mulhalmoni
Neith
Ngame
Pasiphae
Pele
Rán
Rhiannon
Samovila
Scathach
Tabiti
Tawaret
Teteoinnan
Tiamat
Tlalteuctli
Yondung Halmoni

LIGHT CRONES

Acpaxapo
Aja
The Akkan
Akonadi
Ala
Ananke
Anapel
Anna Perenna

Antevorta

Arianrhod

Badb

Baubo

Biliku

Brigid

Bugady Musun

Cerridwen

Corn Woman

Elli

Ereshkigal

Ereshkigal

Estsanatlehi

Evaki

Hestia

Kali Ma

Koliada

Kunapipi

Macha

Madre Vieja

Manat

Manea

Mara

Marzanna

Medusa

Meng-Po Niang Niang

Metis

Mokosh

Morrigu

Nana Buluku

Nanshe

Ngame

Ninhursag

The Norns

Nu Kua

Oya

Pele

Saga

Satine

Sekhmet

Shitala

Skadi

Spider Woman

Tozi

Ved'Ma

Vesta

The Zorya

Zywie

DARK CRONES

Baba Yaga

Cailleach

The Erinyes

Hecate

Hel

Izanami

Kali Ma

Krtya

Nirriti

Rangda

Red Tara

Sekhmet

Sheela Na Gig

THREEFOLD GROUPS

Aglaia, Euphrosyne, and Thalia

Al-Uzza, Al-Lat, and Manat

Badb, Macha, and Morrigu

Banba, Fódla and Ériu

Blodeuwedd, Arianrhod, and Cerridwen

The Camenae: Antevorta, Carmenta, and Postvorta

Corn Woman: Corn Maiden, Corn Mother, and Yellow Woman

The Erinyes: Tisiphone, Alecto, and Megaera

Fódla, Ériu, and Banba

Hebe, Hera, and Hecate

The Matronae

The Norns: Urd, Verthandi, and Skuld

Oshun, Oba, and Oya

Parvati, Durga, and Kali Ma

Persephone, Demeter, and Hecate

Tlazolteotl, Teteoinnan, and Tozi

The Zorya: Zorya Utrennyaya, Zorya Vechernyaya, and Zorya Polunochnaya

SEVEN

· · · · · · · · · · ❋ · · · · · · · · · · ·

Regions and Cultures

AFRICA / MIDDLE EAST

Aha Njoku (Nigeria)

Aida Wedo (West Africa)

Aja (West Africa)

Aje (West Africa)

Akonadi (Ghana)

Akwaba (Ghana)

Ala (Nigeria)

Al-Lat (Arabia)

Al-Uzza (Arabia)

Amashilamma (Sumer)

Anapel (Siberia)

Anath (Canaan)

Anuket (Egypt)

Asase Yaa (Ghana)

Asherah (Middle East)

Ashiakle (Africa)

Ashnan (Mesopotamia)

Astarte (Mesopotamia)

Atargatis (Syria)

Atthar (Arabia)

Aziri (Africa)

Bast (Egypt)

Bunzi (Central Africa)

Eka Abassi (Nigeria)

Enekpe (Africa)

Ereshkigal (Mesopotamia)

Erua (Babylonia)

Erzulie (West Africa)

Fravashi (Persia)

Gbadu (Benin)

Gleti (Benin)

Gula (Mesopotamia)

Hathor (Egypt)

Hebat (Mesopotamia)

Hekit (Egypt)

Inanna (Sumer)

Inkosazana (South Africa)

Ishtar (Babylonia)

Isis (Egypt)

Kamrusepas (Mesopotamia)

Lady of Beasts (Middle East)

Lama (Sumer)

Lilith (Mesopotamia)

Ma'at (Egypt)

Mami Wata (Africa)

Mamlambo (South Africa)

Manat (Arabia)

Mawu (Benin)

Mbaba Mwana Waresa (South Africa)

Mboze (Central Africa)

Medusa (Libya)

Meskhenet (Egypt)

Minona (Benin)

Mujaji (South Africa)

Musso Koroni (Africa)

Mut (Egypt)

Nammu (Sumer)

Nana Buluku (Benin)

Nanshe (Babylonia)

Neith (Egypt)

Nekhebet (Egypt)

Nephthys (Egypt)

Ngame (Egypt)

Ningal (Sumer)

Ninhursag (Mesopotamia)

Ninkasi (Sumer)

Ninlil (Sumer)

Ninsun (Mesopotamia)

Ninti (Sumer)

Nut (Egypt)

Oba (West Africa)

Odudua (West Africa)

Oshun (West Africa)

Oya (West Africa)

Renenet (Egypt)

Sekhmet (Egypt)

Seshat (Egypt)

Shamhat (Mesopotamia)

Shekinah (Middle East)

Siduri Sabitu (Babylonia)

Sophia (Middle East)

Tashmetum (Babylon)

Tawaret (Egypt)

Tefnut (Egypt)

Tiamat (Babylonia)

Uttu (Sumer)

Wadjet (Egypt)

Yemaya (West Africa)

ASIA / INDIA

Agemem (Philippines)

Amaterasu Omikami (Japan)

Annapatni (India)

Aryong Jong (Korea)

Ba Ngu' (Indonesia)

Banka-Mundi (India)

Bardaichila (India)

Benten (Japan)

Biliku (India)

Bixia Yuanjin (China)

Black Tara (Tibet)

Blue Tara (Tibet)

Brag-srin-mo (Tibet)

Bugady Musun (Siberia)

Ch'ang O (China)

Chomo-Lung-Ma (Tibet)

Chuang Mu (China)

Chun T'i (China)

Chup Kamui (Japan)

Danu (India)

Devi (India)

Dewi Nawang Sasih (Indonesia)

Durga (India)

Etugen (Mongolia)

Green Tara (Tibet)

Hsi Wang Mu (China)

Inari (Japan)

Indrani (India)

Ista Devata (India)

Izanami (Japan)

Kali Ma (India)

Kamui Fuchi (Japan)

Koevasi (Melanesia)

Krtya (India)

Kuan Yin (China)

Lajja Gauri (India)

Lakshmi (India)

Ma Gu (China)

Matsu (China)

Maya (India)

Meng-Po Niang Niang (China)

Mulhalmoni (Korea)

Nirriti (India)

Nu Kua (China)

Pajau Yan (Vietnam)

Parvati (India)

Po Ino Nogar (Cambodia)

Purandhi (India)

Radha (India)

Rangda (Bali)

Rati (Bali)

Red Tara (Tibet)

Sangiyan Sari (Indonesia)

Saranyu (India)

Sarasvati (India)

Satine (Indonesia)

Sengdroma (Tibet)

Sgeg Mo Ma (Tibet)

Shakti (India)

Shasti (India)

Shitala (India)

Sita (India)

Sura (India)

Tap Tun (Thailand)

Ushas (India)

Uzume (Japan)

Vac (India)

Vasudhara (Nepal)

Wakahirume (Japan)

White Tara (Tibet)

Xi Hou (China)

Yama No Kami (Japan)

Yaoji (China)

Yaya Zakurai (Japan)

Yellow Tara (Tibet)

Yondung Halmoni (Korea)

Yuki Onne (Japan)

Yum Chenmo (Tibet)

CENTRAL AND EASTERN EUROPE

The Akkan (Eastern Europe)

Anahit (Armenia)

Ararat (Turkey)

Arinna (Turkey)

Artimpaasa (Scythia)

Aspelenie (Lithuania)

Astghik (Armenia)

Ausrine (Lithuania)

Baba Yaga (Russia)

Bendis (Thrace)

The Bereginy (Eastern Europe)

Dugnai (Eastern Europe)

Dziewanna (Eastern Europe)

Dzydzilelya (Poland)

Kikimora (Eastern Europe)

Koliada (Eastern Europe)

Kupala (Eastern Europe)

Lada (Eastern Europe)

Leshachikha (Eastern Europe)

Mara (Latvia)

Marzanna (Poland)

Mati-Syra-Zemlya (Eastern Europe)

Mokosh (Ukraine)

Nuneh (Armenia)

Pereplut (Eastern Europe)

Samovila (Eastern Europe)

Saule (Eastern Europe)

Tabiti (Scythia)

Tsovinar (Armenia)

Ved'Ma (Eastern Europe)

Vesna (Eastern Europe)

Vila (Eastern Europe)

Zaria (Eastern Europe)

The Zorya (Eastern Europe)

Zywie (Poland)

MEDITERRANEAN

Abundantia (Rome)

Aglaia (Greece)

Alemona (Rome)

Ananke (Greece)

Angerona (Rome)

Anna Perenna (Rome)

Antevorta (Rome)

Apate (Greece)

Aphrodite (Greece)

Arachne (Greece)

Artemis (Greece)

Astraea (Greece)

Athene (Greece)

Aurora (Rome)

Baubo (Greece)

Bellona (Rome)

Bia (Greece)

Bona Dea (Rome)

Britomartis (Crete)

Calliope (Greece)

Candelifera (Rome)

Carmenta (Rome)

Carna (Rome)

Ceres (Rome)

Circe (Greece)

Copia (Rome)

Cybele (Rome)

Demeter (Greece)

Diana (Rome)

Dike (Greece)

The Erinyes (Greece)

Euphrosyne (Greece)

Eurynome (Greece)

Feronia (Rome)

Flora (Rome)

Fortuna (Rome)

Gaia (Greece)

Hecate (Greece)

Heimarmene (Greece)

Hera (Greece)

Hestia (Greece)

Iris (Greece)

Juno (Rome)

Lamia (Greece)

Leto (Greece)

Lucina (Rome)

Lupa (Rome)

Maia (Greece)

Manea (Italy)

Marica (Rome)

Metis (Greece)

Minerva (Rome)

Nike (Greece)

Oenothea (Greece)

Ops (Rome)

Pasiphae (Crete)

Pax (Rome)

Persephone (Greece)

Pomona (Rome)

Proserpina (Rome)

Psyche (Greece)

Rhea (Greece)

Selene (Greece)

Snake Woman (Crete)

Thalassa (Greece)

Thalia (Greece)

Themis (Greece)

Tyche (Greece)

Uni (Italy)

Venus (Rome)

Vesta (Rome)

Northern Europe / Celtic Realms

Aine (Ireland)

Airmed (Ireland)

Andraste (Celtic regions)

Ardwinna (Celtic regions)

Arianrhod (Wales)

Armathr (Iceland)

Arnamentia (Celtic regions)

Artio (Celtic regions)

Badb (Ireland)

Baduhenna (Scandinavia)

Banba (Ireland)

Beiwe (Finland)

Blodeuwedd (Wales)

Branwen (Wales)

Brigantia (Celtic regions)

Brigid (Ireland)

Cailleach (Scotland)

Canola (Ireland)

Cerridwen (Wales)

Corra (Celtic regions)

Coventina (Celtic regions)

Creddylad (Wales)

Dana (Ireland)

Don (Wales)

Druantia (Celtic regions)

Eir (Scandinavia)

Elli (Scandinavia)

Eostre (Northern Europe)

Epona (Celtic regions)

Erce (Celtic regions)

Ériu (Ireland)

Ertha (Northern Europe)

Flidais (Ireland)

Freya (Scandinavia)

Frigga (Scandinavia)

Gullveig (Scandinavia)

Gunnlod (Scandinavia)

Habondia (Northern Europe)

Haltia (Finland)

Hel (Scandinavia)

Holda (Northern Europe)

Idunn (Scandinavia)

Ilmatar (Finland)

Jord (Scandinavia)

Kipu-Tytto (Finland)

Lofn (Scandinavia)

Macha (Ireland)

Matronae (Northern Europe)

Medb (Ireland)

Mielikki (Finland)

Momu (Scotland)

Morrigu (Ireland)

Nantosuelta (Celtic regions)

Nehallenia (Celtic regions)

The Norns (Scandinavia)

Rán (Scandinavia)

Rhiannon (Wales)

Saga (Scandinavia)

Scathach (Ireland)

Sheela Na Gig (Ireland)

Sif (Scandinavia)

Sigyn (Scandinavia)

Sjöfn (Scandinavia)

Skadi (Scandinavia)

Sól (Scandinavia)

Sulis (Britain)

Tuonetar (Finland)

The Valkyries (Scandinavia)

Vammatar (Finland)

Var (Scandinavia)

Vellamo (Finland)

PACIFIC ISLANDS /
AUSTRALIA

Apakura (Polynesia)

Brogla (Australia)

Faumea (Polynesia)

Haumea (Polynesia)

Hi'iaka (Polynesia)

Hina (Polynesia)

Hine (Polynesia)

Julunggul (Australia)

Kunapipi (Australia)

Mahuika (Polynesia)

The Mar'rallang (Australia)

Marama (Polynesia)

Pani (Polynesia)

Papatuanuku (Polynesia)

Pele (Polynesia)

THE AMERICAS

Acpaxapo (Mesoamerica)

Akewa (South America)

Akhushtal (Mesoamerica)

Atira (Native America)

Auchimalgen (South America)

Axomama (South America)

Bachué (South America)

Caipora (South America)

Chalchiuhtlicue (Mesoamerica)

Chantico (Mesoamerica)

Chasca (South America)

Chicomecoatl (Mesoamerica)

Chihucoatl (Mesoamerica)

Coatlicue (Mesoamerica)

Cocomama (South America)

Corn Woman (Native America)

Coyolxauhqui (Mesoamerica)

Estsanatlehi (Native America)

Evaki (South America)

Gyhldeptis (Native America)

Itzpapalotl (Mesoamerica)

Ix Chel (Mesoamerica)

Ixtab (Mesoamerica)

Madre Vieja (Mesoamerica)

Malinalxochitl (Mesoamerica)

Mama Allpa (South America)

Mama Cocha (South America)

Mama Oello (South America)

Mama Quilla (South America)

Mayahuel (Mesoamerica)

Onatha (Native America)

Pachamama (South America)

Pinga (Native America)

Pukkeenegak (Native America)

Sedna (Native America)

Spider Woman (Native America)

Teteoinnan (Mesoamerica)

Tlalteuctli (Mesoamerica)

Tlazolteotl (Mesoamerica)

Tozi (Mesoamerica)

White Buffalo Calf Woman (Native America)

Xochiquetzal (Mesoamerica)

Zaramama (South America)

BIBLIOGRAPHY

· · · · · · · · · · · ✳ · · · · · · · · · · ·

Adler, Margot. *Drawing Down the Moon.* New York: Penguin, 1986.

Andrews, Tamra. *Dictionary of Nature Myths: Legends of Earth, Sea, and Sky.* New York: Oxford University Press, 2000.

Ann, Martha, and Dorothy Myers Imel. *Goddesses in World Mythology: A Biographical Dictionary.* New York: Oxford University Press, 1993.

Ashby, Muata. *African Religion, Vol. 1-5.* Miami: Sema Institute, 2005.

Bell, Robert E. *Women of Classical Mythology—A Bibliographical Dictionary.* New York: Oxford University Press, 1993.

Bienkowski, Piotr, and Alan Millard, eds. *Dictionary of the Ancient Near East.* Philadelphia: University of Pennsylvania Press, 2000.

Bolen, Jean Shinoda. *Goddesses in Everywoman : Powerful Archetypes in Women's Lives.* 20th anniversary edition. New York: Harper-Collins, 2004.

Budapest, Zsuzsanna. *The Holy Book of Women's Mysteries.* Oakland, CA: Wingbow Press, 1989.

Cirlot, J. E. *A Dictionary of Symbols.* New York: Philosophical Library, 1983.

Condren, Mary. *The Serpent and the Goddess: Women, Religion, and Power in Celtic Ireland.* New edition. Dublin, Ireland: New Island Books, 2002.

Conway, D. J. *Maiden, Mother, Crone: The Myth and Reality of the Triple Goddess.* St. Paul, MN: Llewellyn, 1995.

———. *The Magick of the Gods and Goddesses: How to Invoke their Powers.* St. Paul, MN: Llewellyn, 1997.

———. *Moon Magick: Myth & Magick, Crafts & Recipes, Rituals & Spells.* St. Paul, MN: Llewellyn, 1995.

Cunningham, Scott. *Wicca: A Guide for the Solitary Practitioner.* St. Paul, MN: Llewellyn, 1993

———. *Living Wicca: A Further Guide for the Solitary Practitioner.* St. Paul, MN: Llewellyn, 2002.

———. *Magical Aromatherapy.* St. Paul, MN: Llewellyn, 1989.

Curtis, Vesta Sarkhosh. *Persian Myths.* Austin, TX: University of Texas Press, 1993.

Dallapiccola, A. L. *Hindu Myths.* Austin, TX: University of Texas Press, 2003.

De Vita, Alexis Brooks. *Mythatypes: Signatures and Signs of African/ Diaspora and Black Goddesses.* Westport, CT: Greenwood Press, 2000.

Echlin, Kim. *Inanna: From the Myths of Ancient Sumer.* Toronto: Groundwood Books, 2003.

Eisler, Riane. *The Chalice and the Blade.* New York: HarperOne, 1988.

Estes, Clarissa Pinkola. *Women Who Run with the Wolves: Myths and Stories of the Wild Woman Archetype*. New York: Ballantine Books, 1992.

Frymer-Kensky, Tikva. *In the Wake of the Goddess: Women, Culture and the Biblical Transformation of Pagan Myth*. New York: Ballantine Books, 1993.

Gadon, Elinor. *The Once and Future Goddess: A Sweeping Visual Chronicle of the Sacred Female and Her Reemergence in the Cult*. New York: HarperOne, 1989.

Gimbutas, Marija. *The Language of the Goddess*. London: Thames & Hudson, 2001.

———. *The Living Goddesses*. Berkeley, CA: University of California Press, 2001.

———. *The Goddesses and Gods of Old Europe: Myths and Cult Images*. New edition. Berkeley, CA: University of California Press, 1982.

George, Demetra. *Mysteries of the Dark Moon: The Healing Power of the Dark Goddess*. San Francisco: HarperOne, 1992.

Gossen, Gary H., ed. *South and Meso-American Native Spirituality: From the Cult of the Feathered Serpent to the Theology of Liberation*. New York: Herder & Herder, 1997.

Graves, Robert. *The White Goddess: A Historical Grammar of Poetic Myth*. New York: Farrar, Straus and Giroux, 1979.

———. *The Greek Myths*. New York: Penguin, 1993

Guiley, Rosemary Ellen. *The Encyclopedia of Witches and Witchcraft*. New York: Facts on File, 1990.

Hinnells, John R., ed. *A Handbook of Ancient Religions*. New York: Cambridge University Press, 2007.

The Holy Bible. NIV Edition. Grand Rapids, MI: Zondervan, 2002.

Johnson, Buffie. *Lady of the Beasts: The Goddess and Her Sacred Animals*. Second revised edition. Rochester, VT: Inner Traditions, 1994.

Jung, C. G. *The Archetypes and the Collective Unconscious*. Trans. Gerhard Adler and R. F. C. Hull. Second edition. Princeton, NJ: Princeton University Press, 1981.

Kramer, Samuel Noah. *Sumerian Mythology: A Study of Spiritual and Literary Achievement in the Third Millennium B.C.* New York: Harper, 1961.

Larrington, Carolyn, trans. *The Poetic Edda*. New edition. New York: Oxford University Press, 1999.

Laura, Judith. *Goddess Spirituality for the 21st Century: From Kabbalah to Quantum Physics*. Kensington, MD: Open Sea Press, 1997.

Marashinsky, Amy Sophia. *The Goddess Oracle: A Way to Wholeness through the Goddess and Ritual*. Boston: Element Books, 1997.

Mason, Colin. *A Short History of Asia*. Second edition. New York: Palgrave Macmillan, 2005.

Mitchell, Stephen. *Gilgamesh: A New English Version*. New York: Free Press, 2006.

Monaghan, Patricia. *The Book of Goddesses & Heroines*. St. Paul, MN: Llewellyn, 1993.

———.*The Goddess Path: Myths, Invocations, and Rituals*. St. Paul, MN: Llewellyn, 1999.

———. *The Goddess Companion: Daily Meditations on the Goddess*. St. Paul, MN: Llewellyn, 1999.

Morwyn. *Magic From Brazil*. Second edition. St. Paul, MN: Llewellyn, 2001.

Mountainwater, Shekinah. *Ariadne's Thread: A Workbook of Goddess Magick*. Freedom, CA: Crossing Press, 1991.

Olson, Carl, ed. *Book of the Goddess Past and Present: An Introduction to Her Religion*. Long Grove, IL: Waveland Press, 2002.

Pomeroy, Sarah B. *Goddesses, Whores, Wives, and Slaves: Women in Classical Antiquity*. New York: Schocken, 1995.

Rabinowitz, Jacob. *The Faces of God: Canaanite Mythology as Hebrew Theology*. New York: Spring Publishing, 1998.

Redmond, Layne. *When Drummers Were Women*. New York: Three Rivers Press, 1997.

Reed, Ellen Cannon. *The Witches Tarot*. St. Paul, MN: Llewellyn, 1989.

Rolleston, T. W. *Celtic Myths and Legends*. New York: Dover Publications, 1990.

Rountree, Kathry. *Embracing the Witch and the Goddess: Feminist Ritual-Makers in New Zealand*. London: Routledge, 2003.

Smith, Huston. *The World's Religions: Our Great Wisdom Traditions*. San Francisco: HarperOne, 1991.

Starhawk. *The Spiral Dance: A Rebirth of Ancient Religion of the Great Goddess*. San Francisco: Harper & Row, 1979.

Stone, Merlin. *Ancient Mirrors of Womanhood: A Treasury of Goddess and Heroine Lore from around the World*. Boston: Beacon Press, 1990.

———. *When God Was a Woman*. New York: Harcourt Brace Jovanovich, 1976.

Telesco, Patricia. *365 Goddess: A Daily Guide to the Magic and Inspiration of the Goddess*. New York: HarperOne, 1998.

Telyndru, Jhenah. *Avalon Within: Inner Sovereignty and Personal Transformation through the Avalonian Mysteries*. Charleston, SC: BookSurge Press, 2005.

Turnbull, Sharon. *Goddess Gift: Discover Your Personal Goddess Type*. Los Angeles: Quiet Time Press, 2007.

Virtue, Doreen. *Goddess Guidance Oracle Cards*. Carlsbad, CA: Hay House, 2004.

Wade-Gayles, Gloria. *My Soul is a Witness: African-American Women's Spirituality*. Boston: Beacon Press, 2002.

Walker, Barbara G. *The Women's Encyclopedia of Myths and Secrets*. New York: Harper & Row, 1983.

———. *The Woman's Dictionary of Symbol's and Sacred Objects*. San Francisco: Harper & Row, 1988.

Warner, Elizabeth. *Russian Myths*. Austin, TX: University of Texas Press, 2002.

Wauters, Ambika. *Chakras and their Archetypes: Uniting Energy Awareness and Spiritual Growth*. Berkeley, CA: Crossing Press, 1997.

Wolfe, Amber. *In the Shadow of the Shaman*. St. Paul, MN: Llewellyn, 1988.

———. *Personal Alchemy: A Handbook of Healing and Self-Transformation*. St. Paul, MN: Llewellyn, 1993.

The World Book Encyclopedia, 2007 edition. Chicago: World Book, 2007.

INDEX

· · · · · · · · · · · ✳ · · · · · · · · · · ·

C

F

G

H

M

R

 LLEWELLYN ORDERING INFORMATION

Order Online:
Visit our website at www.llewellyn.com, select your books, and order them on our secure server.

Order by Phone:
- Call toll-free within the U.S. at 1-877-NEW-WRLD (1-877-639-9753). Call toll-free within Canada at 1-866-NEW-WRLD (1-866-639-9753)
- We accept VISA, MasterCard, and American Express

Order by Mail:
Send the full price of your order (MN residents add 6.5% sales tax) in U.S. funds, plus postage & handling to:

Llewellyn Worldwide
2143 Wooddale Drive, Dept. 978-0-7387-1551-3
Woodbury, MN 55125-2989

Postage & Handling:
Standard (U.S., Mexico, & Canada). If your order is:
$24.99 and under, add $3.00
$25.00 and over, FREE STANDARD SHIPPING

AK, HI, PR: $15.00 for one book plus $1.00 for each additional book.

International Orders (airmail only):
$16.00 for one book plus $3.00 for each additional book

Orders are processed within 2 business days.
Please allow for normal shipping time. Postage and handling rates subject to change.

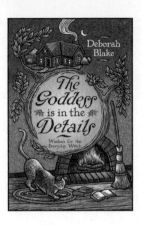

The Goddess is in the Details

Wisdom for the Everyday Witch

DEBORAH BLAKE

Being a Witch isn't limited to casting a spell under the full moon or consecrating a ritual circle. Whether you're calling the Goddess or doing the dishes, your wonderfully Witchy ways are woven into everything you do.

With her signature down-to-earth wisdom and warmth, Deborah Blake takes you into the heart of what it means to be a Witch all day, every day. Filled with practical suggestions and useful advice, this essential book covers all aspects of the modern Witch's life: the seven core beliefs of Witches, mindful eating and health, creating sacred space at home, relationships with non-Pagans, sex and the single Witch, raising Pagan children, solitary and coven practice, and green living.

978-0-7387-1486-8 • 240 pages • $16.95

To order, call 1-877-NEW-WRLD
Prices subject to change without notice
Order at Llewellyn.com 24 hours a day, 7 days a week!

Goddess Afoot!

Practicing Magic with Celtic & Norse Goddesses

MICHELLE SKYE

Written in the same warm, practical style as *Goddess Alive!*, this book takes you further along on your spiritual path to the Goddess. With this guide, you'll discover how to use spellwork and magic to make lasting changes in your life. You'll learn how to attune to a specific goddess for inspiration and empowerment, and connect with the energy of that goddess to manifest your dreams and desires.

Each chapter starts with a goddess from the Norse or Celtic pantheons, and presents her myths, a pathworking, a guided meditation, an invocation, and three magical activities or crafts. Twelve powerful goddesses offer assistance in a variety of ways, from helping you attract abundance to becoming more psychic. You can gain balance in your life with Cymidei Cymeinfoll, the Welsh goddess of war and birth; learn to take risks with Cessair, the founding goddess of Ireland; and allow yourself to shine with Sunna, the Norse goddess of the sun.

978-0-7387-1331-1 • 312 pages • $19.95

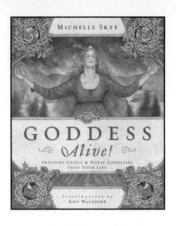

Goddess Alive!

Inviting Celtic & Norse Goddesses into Your Life

MICHELLE SKYE

The seasons, moon phases, and even our personal experiences can be linked to the Divine Feminine. They have a face . . . they have a name . . . they have a goddess!

Meet thirteen vibrant Celtic and Norse goddesses very much alive in today's world. Explore each deity's unique mythology and see how she relates to Sabbats and moon rites. Lyrical meditations will guide you to other-worldly realms where you'll meet Danu, the Irish mother goddess of wisdom, and Freya, the Norse goddess of love and war. As you progress spiritually, you'll begin to see Aine in the greening of the trees and recognize Brigid in a seed's life-giving potential.

Goddess Alive! also includes crafts, invocation rituals, and other magical activities to help you connect with each goddess.

978-0-7387-1080-8 • 288 pages • $18.95

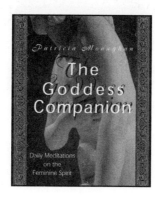

Goddess Companion

Daily Meditations on the Feminine Spirit

Patricia Monaghan

Engage your feminine spirit! Here are hundreds of authentic goddess prayers, invocations, chants, and songs—one for each day of the year. They come from dozens of sources, ranging from the great classical European authors Ovid and Horace, to the marvelously passionate Hindu poets Ramprasad and Ramakrishna, to the anonymous gifted poets who first composed the folksongs of Lithuania, West Africa, and Alaska. In fresh, contemporary language that maintains the spirit of the originals, these prayers can be used for personal meditation, for private or public ritual, or for your own creative inspiration. They capture the depth of feeling, the philosophical complexity, and the ecological awareness of goddess cultures the world over.

Organized as a daily meditation book, *The Goddess Companion* is also indexed by culture, goddess, and subject, so you can easily find prayers for specific purposes. Following each prayer is a thoughtfully written piece of prose, which illustrates the aspects of the Goddess working in our everyday lives.

978-1-56718-463-1 • 400 pages • $17.95

The Goddess Path

Myths, Invocations & Rituals

PATRICIA MONAGHAN

For some, finding the Goddess is a private intellectual search, with speculation on her meaning in culture and myth. For others, she is an emotional construct, a way of understanding the varying voices of the emerging self. Then there are those for whom she is part of everyday ritual, honored in meditation and prayer. All are on the Goddess path.

If you have never encountered the Goddess outside your own heart, this book will introduce you to some of her manifestations. If you have long been on this path, it will provide prayers and rituals to stimulate your celebrations. *The Goddess Path* offers a creative approach to worship, one in which you can develop and ritualize your own distinctive connection to her many manifestations from around the world.

978-1-56718-467-9 • 288 pages • $16.95

One Witch's Way

A Magical Year of Stories, Spells & Such

BRONWYNN FORREST TORGERSON

The Wheel of the Year is given a fresh spin in this inspiring ode to the Wiccan life. Month by month, Bronwynn Forrest Torgerson invigorates Pagan principles with rituals, songs, spells, and poetry. But the underlying thread of this whimsical Wiccan tapestry is Torgerson's own personal stories—funny, enthralling, and moving—that illuminate one Witch's way.

This rich collection offers spiritual lessons, belly laughs, and heartfelt wisdom to Witches everywhere. Mingling the practical and the personal, Torgerson explores journeys in January, love and transformation in February, communion in June, and the power of song in September. Between lyrical verses and original parables, you'll witness the author's joys, struggles, minor miracles, and thrilling encounters with the divine. From the mundane (magickally finding the perfect apartment) to the mystical (receiving guidance from the gods), Torgerson recounts the sacred forces that have shaped one Witch's life.

978-0-7387-1369-4 • 264 pages • $15.95

Maiden, Mother, Crone

The Myth and Reality of the Triple Goddess

D. J. Conway

The Triple Goddess is with every one of us each day of our lives. In our inner journeys toward spiritual evolution, each woman and man goes through the stages of maiden (infant to puberty), mother (adult and parent), and crone (aging elder). *Maiden, Mother, Crone* is a guide to the myths and interpretations of the Great Goddess archetype and her three faces, so that we may better understand and more peacefully accept the cycle of birth and death.

Learning to interpret the symbolic language of the myths is important to spiritual growth, for the symbols are part of the map that guides each of us to the Divine Center. By learning the true meaning of the ancient symbols, through facing the cycles of life, and by following the meditations and simple rituals provided in this book, women and men alike can translate these ancient teachings into personal revelations.

Not all goddesses can be conveniently divided into the clear aspects of maiden, mother, and crone. This book covers these goddesses as well, including the Fates, the Muses, Valkyries, and others.

978-0-875-42171-1 • 240 pages • $14.95

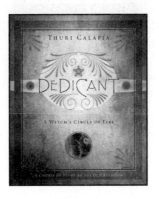

Dedicant

A Witch's Circle of Fire

THURI CALAFIA

This comprehensive course is a lifeline for solitary seekers, providing guidance through a full year and a day of Wiccan study.

Experienced teacher Thuri Calafia introduces monthly lessons that follow the Wheel of the Year. As the earth's cycles unfold, you'll explore historical lore, Sabbat rituals, seasonal energy, tools, and symbols associated with each time of the year. Both practical and spiritual aspects of Wicca are discussed, including etiquette, spellcasting, herb work, ritual garb, selecting a teacher or coven, choosing a magical name, and more. Each lesson—filled with meditations, rituals, pathworking exercises, activities, ethics issues, and personal anecdotes from the author—will draw you closer to the Path of the Wise and prepare you for the next step in your Wiccan education.

Dedicant kicks off a four-volume Wiccan study series—Dedicant, Initiate, Adept, and Master—based on the traditional degree system.

978-0-7387-1328-1 • 360 pages • $19.95

Natural Witchery

Intuitive, Personal & Practical Magick

ELLEN DUGAN

Natural Witchery offers dozens of ways to hone your intuition, enhance your magickal powers, and enliven your everyday practice.

Ellen Dugan goes to the heart of what it means to be a natural Witch. Forget about lineage, degrees, and politically correct titles. Her thoughtful observations and wise words will guide you back to what's important: forging your own unique spiritual path. These engaging exercises will help you look within yourself and stretch your psychic talents, discover your elemental strengths, and charge up your personal power.

Dugan's personal anecdotes and humor liven up the lessons and keep you grounded throughout the daily joys and trials of life as a natural Witch.

978-0-7387-0922-2 • 288 pages • $16.95

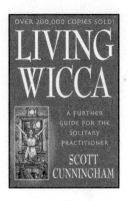

Living Wicca
A Further Guide for the Solitary Practitioner

Scott Cunningham

Living Wicca is for those who have made the conscious decision to bring their Wiccan spirituality into their everyday lives. It provides solitary practitioners with the tools and added insights that will help them blaze their own spiritual paths—to become their own high priests and priestesses.

Living Wicca takes a philosophical look at the questions, practices, and differences within Witchcraft. It covers the various tools of learning available to the practitioner, the importance of secrecy in one's practice, guidelines to performing ritual when ill, magical names, initiation, and the Mysteries. It discusses the benefits of daily prayer and meditation, making offerings to the gods, how to develop a prayerful attitude, and how to perform Wiccan rites when away from home or in emergency situations.

Unlike any other book on the subject, *Living Wicca* is a step-by-step guide to creating your own Wiccan tradition and personal vision of the gods, designing your personal ritual and symbols, developing your own book of shadows, and truly living your Craft.

978-0875-42184-1 • 240 pages • $12.95

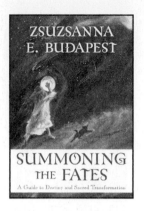

Summoning the Fates

A Guide to Destiny and
Sacred Transformation

ZSUZSANNA E. BUDAPEST

During the 1956 Hungarian Revolution, Z. Budapest narrowly escaped a massacre. Was it chance that spared her life, or destiny?

Budapest, a pioneer of the women's spirituality movement, introduces us to the three Fates that rule our lives. Not even the gods and goddesses can escape these raw forces of nature presiding over the past, present, and future. Budapest uses fairy tales, historical lore, and personal anecdotes to describe the three sacred sisters who are especially active during our thirty-year life cycles: Urdh (youth), Verdandi (adulthood), and Skuld (the crone years).

Want a taste of the cosmic soup bubbling in Fate's cauldron? Budapest also offers heartfelt advice, exercises, and rituals to help you connect with the Fates and embrace your own unique destiny.

978-0-7387-1083-9 • 288 pages • $15.95